Ambiguous Loss

AMBIGUOUS LOSS

Learning to Live with Unresolved Grief

Pauline Boss

HARVARD UNIVERSITY PRESS
Cambridge, Massachusetts
London, England
1999

LIBRARY OF CONGRESS CATALOGING-IN-PUBLICATION DATA

Boss, Pauline.
Ambiguous loss : learning to live with unresolved grief /
Pauline Boss.
p. cm.
Includes bibliographical references.
ISBN 0-674-01738-2 (alk. paper)
1. Loss (Psychology). 2. Grief. 3. Family—Psychological aspects.
4. Interpersonal relations. I. Title.
BF575.D35B67 1999
155.9'3—dc21   98-50585

For Ellie

Contents

1   Frozen Grief   1

2   Leaving without Goodbye   26

3   Goodbye without Leaving   45

4   Mixed Emotions   61

5   Ups and Downs   77

6   The Family Gamble   93

7   The Turning Point   106

8   Making Sense out of Ambiguity   118

9   The Benefit of a Doubt   133

Notes   143

Acknowledgments   153

Ambiguous Loss

⚞ 1 ⚟

Frozen Grief

I GREW UP IN A MIDWESTERN IMMIGRANT COMMUNITY where everyone I looked up to came from someplace else. Parents and grandparents had crossed the Atlantic in the early 1900s to find a better life in the fertile valleys of southern Wisconsin. But it wasn't always better, because ties had been severed with beloved family members back in Switzerland. Letters came at least until World War II, but they were bittersweet. They always ended with lines like "Will we ever see each other again?" I remember my father being melancholy for days after he got a letter from his mother or brother. And my maternal grandmother pined ceaselessly for her mother back in her homeland. She knew they would never meet again because poverty and then World War II prevented travel. Homesickness became a central part of my family's culture. I never really knew who was in or out of our family—or where home really was. Was it in the old country or the new? Were these people I had never seen or met really my family? I did not know them but I was keenly aware that my father and grandmother did. Many times their thoughts

2   seemed far away. Their losses of beloved family members were never resolved, and so those who lived with them also experienced the ambiguity of absence and presence.

What I as a child thought was my Walton-like family on a farm in southern Wisconsin was not the family portrait my father or my maternal grandmother would have painted. Their version of family would have included people I had never met—relatives across the Atlantic who existed only in their memories. Because part of what they thought of as "family" was always out of physical reach, and because we lived in a community where immigrants were numerous, homesickness was considered normal. Longing for faraway family members was so common that at an early age I became curious about this unnamed loss and the melancholy that never went away. It was all around me. Many times I heard my father with his heavy accent telling young foreigners who came for his counsel, "Don't stay away from your homeland more than three months or you'll never again know where home is." I wondered what he meant.

For more than forty years, I remained rooted in that immigrant community, the village of my birth, commuting to the nearby University of Wisconsin in Madison when I became a student there and, later, a professor. When I finally uprooted myself, I understood my father's words. Even though my move to the Twin Cities of Minneapolis and St. Paul was minor compared with his, I too became confused about where home was. Not only did I think a lot about the folks back home, but I refused to sell my house there and kept it furnished—as if I were coming back at any moment. But as time went on, I could see that a big city offered adventure and excitement. I set about finding a new home—a small carriage-house loft—and new friends. My children came to visit during their breaks from college and work, and I talked often on the phone with my sister and mother. With such opportunities for visits, homesickness was short-lived. I became clear about where I wanted to be even though everyone in my family was someplace else.

Although I always felt some misgivings about what I had lost by leaving my hometown, they did not immobilize me. Things were easier for me than for my elders because my immediate family ties were not cut off by poverty and world war. Nevertheless, the move from village to metropolis was a shock. At my vulnerable moments, my family was "there" for me. One day I found in front of my mailbox a heavy package wrapped in brown paper, tied with butcher cord, and stamped with a massive amount of postage. It was a shoebox full of my father's home-grown potatoes. "Make some soup," my mother wrote. "It will help make you feel at home there." And it did.

The family that exists in people's minds is more important than the one recorded in the census taker's notebook, especially when family members are increasingly separated and on the move because of work demands, unemployment, domestic break-ups, war, or simply their own choices. The immigration experience provides special insights into how people learn to let go of what used to be in order to embrace the new. Personal narratives illustrate the bittersweet legacy of ambiguity about psychological presence and absence for immigrant families, especially when the psychological family is not in accord with the physically present family. Unless people resolve the ambiguous loss—the incomplete or uncertain loss—that is inherent in uprooting, and bring into

4   some congruence their psychological and physical families, the legacy of frozen grief may affect their offspring for generations to come, compounding itself as more ordinary losses inevitably occur.[1] This is the legacy of immigration and migration that lies at the root of many personal and family problems.

As a researcher and a family therapist, I have worked with more than four thousand families, and am convinced that families are psychological as well as physical entities. What I look for is some degree of congruence between the physical and the psychological constructions of family, for without knowing who is perceived as absent or present in both cases, children and adults may not function optimally. Without knowing who is routinely and fully *there* for them as family, people find it difficult to function normally.

In a sense I use the word "family" loosely, but my criteria are nonetheless rigorous. By family I mean that intimate group of people whom we can count on over time for comfort, care, nurturance, support, sustenance, and emotional closeness. Family can be people with whom we grew up—called the family of origin—or it can be people we select in adulthood—called the family of choice. The latter may include biological or nonbiological offspring or no offspring at all. Instead, we might be an "auntie" or an "uncle" to a relative's or friend's children, or the stepparent to a partner's child. This view of family stresses the criterion of being present—psychologically and physically—even more than that of being biologically related.

We aren't always absolutely clear about *who is family*, even in our own families. The composition of the family keeps changing in the minds of family members as conditions change and losses and additions occur. The real family is often not obvious to outsiders, but who's in and who's out is something that the professional therapists who work with couples and families need to know. When people experience ambiguous losses, causing confusion and distress, the psychological family becomes especially important in efforts to minimize the pain. Yet there must be some congruence between the psychological and the physical if families are to function well.

Although the clinical literature has been mostly silent on ambiguous loss, the phenomenon has always been the stuff of opera, literature, and the theater. In these genres, losses that remain vague and uncertain are embellished. Homer's Penelope waits for her missing husband; Arthur Miller's father in *All My Sons* insists his son is alive long after a fatal air crash. We romanticize what we cannot understand and take pleasure from stories about the waiting of Odysseus' wife and Puccini's Butterfly. The very situations that people least understand stir their unconscious. For the one who experiences it, however, the ambiguity of waiting and wondering is anything but romantic. Ambiguous loss is always stressful and often tormenting. Information about it belongs in the literature of psychotherapy as well as in the arts. Perhaps the reason that few, except artists, have written about ambiguous loss is that it is so common in people's lives. To be sure, the phenomenon is not new, but the explicit labeling and describing of it on the basis of clinical research and observation is new.

Of all the losses experienced in personal relationships, ambiguous loss is the most devastating because it remains

6   unclear, indeterminate. An old English nursery rhyme encap-
sulates the distressing feeling of uncertainty:

> As I was walking up the stair,
> I met a man who was not there.
> He was not there again today.
> Oh, how I wish he'd go away.

Here we see the absurdity of not being certain about a person's absence or presence. People hunger for certainty. Even sure knowledge of death is more welcome than a continuation of doubt.

Consider an old woman in Bosnia hugging a fleshless skull that she takes for her son, on the sketchy evidence of a familiar shoe found nearby. This woman is suffering from a unique kind of loss that defies closure, in which the status of a loved one as "there" or "not there" remains indefinitely unclear. One cannot tell for sure if the loved one is dead or alive, dying or recovering, absent or present. Not only is there a lack of information regarding the person's whereabouts, there is no official or community verification that anything is lost—no death certificate, no wake or sitting shiva, no funeral, no body, nothing to bury. The uncertainty makes ambiguous loss the most distressful of all losses, leading to symptoms that are not only painful but often missed or misdiagnosed. Open any newspaper and you'll find a story of this unique kind of loss—an airplane crash in a Florida swamp leaving families devastated because the bodies of their loved ones cannot be found, or a mother hanging yellow ribbons for her son who mysteriously disappeared over a decade ago, or the child of a pilot shot down somewhere over southeast Asia still hoping he will come walking out of the jungle some day. Ambiguous

loss always results from war and violence, but it works even 7
more insidiously in everyday life. Mates leave, children leave,
coworkers get fired, parents grow old and absent-minded.
Our hunger for absolute certainty is rarely satisfied even in the
relationships we believe are permanent and predictable.

Ambiguous loss can cause personal and family problems,
not because of flaws in the psyches of those experiencing the
loss, but because of situations beyond their control or outside
constraints that block the coping and grieving processes.
Therapy based on the recognition of the ambiguity of the loss
frees people to understand, cope, and move on after the loss,
even if it remains unclear. The major theoretical premise
underlying therapy is this: the greater the ambiguity surrounding one's loss, the more difficult it is to master it and the
greater one's depression, anxiety, and family conflict.

Perceiving loved ones as present when they are physically
gone, or perceiving them as gone when they are physically
present, can make people feel helpless and thus more prone to
depression, anxiety, and relationship conflicts.[2] How does
ambiguous loss do this? First, because the loss is confusing,
people are baffled and immobilized. They don't know how to
make sense of the situation. They can't problem-solve because
they do not yet know whether the problem (the loss) is final or
temporary. If the uncertainty continues, families often respond with absolutes, either acting as if the person is completely gone, or denying that anything has changed. Neither is
satisfactory. Second, the uncertainty prevents people from ad-
justing to the ambiguity of their loss by reorganizing the roles
and rules of their relationship with the loved one, so that the
couple or family relationship freezes in place. If they have not
already closed out the person who is missing physically or psy-

8   chologically, they hang on to the hope that things will return to the way they used to be. Third, people are denied the symbolic rituals that ordinarily support a clear loss—such as a funeral after a death in the family. Few if any supportive rituals exist for people experiencing ambiguous loss. Their experience remains unverified by the community around them, so that there is little validation of what they are experiencing and feeling. Fourth, the absurdity of ambiguous loss reminds people that life is not always rational and just; consequently, those who witness it tend to withdraw rather than give neighborly support, as they would do in the case of a death in the family. Finally, because ambiguous loss is a loss that goes on and on, those who experience it tell me they become physically and emotionally exhausted from the relentless uncertainty.

With this special kind of loss, the ambiguity can stem either from a lack of information about the loss or from conflicting perceptions about *which* family members people see as absent or present in their intimate circle. For example, children of a soldier missing in action have no information about the whereabouts of their father and don't know if he is dead or alive, but children in a divorced family may know where their father is, even see him, yet disagree with their mother as to whether or not he is still part of their family.

There are two basic kinds of ambiguous loss. In the first type, people are perceived by family members as *physically absent* but psychologically present, because it's unclear whether they are dead or alive. Missing soldiers and kidnapped children illustrate this type of loss in its catastrophic form. More everyday occurrences include losses within divorced and adoptive families, where a parent or child is viewed as absent or missing.

In the second type of ambiguous loss, a person is perceived
as physically present but *psychologically absent*. This condition is illustrated in the extreme by people with Alzheimer's
disease, addictions, and other chronic mental illnesses. It can
also occur when a person experiences serious head trauma,
first becoming comatose and then waking up a different
person. In more everyday situations, people who are exces-
sively preoccupied with their work or other outside interests
also fit this category.

Both types of ambiguous loss, their effects, and how people
live with them are discussed in subsequent chapters, but first,
ambiguous loss and reactions to it must be more clearly
differentiated from ordinary loss.

In both types of ambiguous loss, those who suffer the loss
have to deal with something very different from ordinary,
clear-cut loss. The most obvious ordinary loss is death, an
event codified by official verification—a death certificate, a
funeral ceremony, and a ritualized burial, entombment, or
scattering of the ashes. In the case of a death, everybody
agrees that a permanent loss has occurred and that mourning can begin. The great majority of people deal with such
a loss by what we might call normal grieving. In normal
grieving, as Sigmund Freud wrote in 1917 in "Mourning
and Melancholia," the goal of recovery is to relinquish one's
ties to the loved object (person) and eventually invest in a
new relationship. This is the difficult work of mourning, but
it is a process that is meant to end. From this perspective,
people who are emotionally healthy are expected to resolve
a loss and move on to new relationships—and to do so
relatively quickly.

But a few people react even to clear-cut losses with what
Freud called pathological melancholia, and what therapists

10 today usually call melancholia or complicated grieving, in which a person remains stuck on and preoccupied with the lost object. Examples are a widow's refusal to eat, an orphaned child's temper tantrums, and a widower's reclusive behavior.

In the case of ambiguous loss, however, melancholia, or complicated grieving, can be a normal reaction to a complicated situation—the endless searching of a battlefield by the mother of a missing soldier; a stepchild's angry outbursts when his biological parent is totally excluded; a wife's depression and withdrawal because her husband has suffered a brain injury and is no longer himself. The inability to resolve such ambiguous losses is due to the *outside* situation, not to internal personality defects. And the outside force that freezes the grief is the uncertainty and ambiguity of the loss.

When people suffering ambiguous loss seek treatment and are evaluated in the traditional way, they often look dysfunctional, exhibiting readily diagnosed symptoms such as anxiety, depression, and somatic illnesses. The question that therapists and physicians should add to their diagnostic repertoire is this: Is the patient experiencing any ambiguous losses that might account for his or her immobilization? Even in otherwise healthy people, the uncertainty of such a loss can diminish power and get in the way of action.

Surely, people with unclear losses should not blame themselves—or other family members—for their frozen grief. Nor should clinicians limit their assessment to the internal dynamics of the patient. Unlike death, an ambiguous loss may never allow people to achieve the detachment that is necessary for normal closure. Just as ambiguity complicates loss, it complicates the mourning process. People can't start grieving because the situation is indeterminate. It feels like a loss but it is not *really* one. The confusion freezes the grieving process. People plummet from hope to hopelessness and back again. Depression, anxiety, and somatic illnesses often set in. The symptoms affect the individuals first, but can radiate in a ripple effect that impacts the whole family, as people are ignored or, worse yet, abandoned. Family members can become so preoccupied with the loss that they withdraw from one another. The family becomes a system with nobody in it.

This scenario, of course, plays out in varying degrees of severity, depending on the family and the nature of the loss. To see how ambiguous loss can affect a contemporary family, let us consider the problems of Mr. and Mrs. Johnson, who though not debilitated were becoming increasingly distant.

Mr. Johnson, a corporate executive in a large firm, called me to see if he could bring his wife in for therapy. A psychiatrist was treating Mrs. Johnson with medication for her depression and had recommended family therapy as well. When the couple arrived for their first visit, it was as if there were two strangers in the room. They did not interact with each other at all, but only interacted with me. They both reported feelings of confusion about their marriage and "couldn't sort it out." "Our marriage is a façade—there's no warmth anymore," said Mrs. Johnson. It emerged that she had felt alone for many years. Mr. Johnson was out of town much of the time or stayed long hours at the office. She never knew when or if he was coming home. When he did come home, she said, "He's extremely busy; he doesn't talk about anything and doesn't ask about my life or the children. I volunteer the information but he doesn't seem interested." About a year ago, she confronted him about his absence and he exploded, "My career *is*

12 more rewarding than our relationship; I'd *rather* be traveling!" She was devastated and since then has become increasingly depressed, barely making it through the day. Their two children are now in high school, needing her less and appearing only briefly in the kitchen before disappearing into their private bedrooms to their own TVs, their own computers, and their own telephones. In addition, after some probing, Mrs. Johnson revealed that her mother was also "leaving her" because she was "slipping away into dementia."

The Johnson family was full of ambiguous losses. Although neither husband nor wife could name what they were experiencing beyond the depressive symptoms that were so obvious in Mrs. Johnson, the ambiguous losses in this family were insidiously taking their toll on everyone. The marriage was empty and so was the family. To ease Mrs. Johnson's depression, the system would have to change (her children were willing, her husband was not, her mother could not be)—or she would have to change and learn to accept the ambiguity that surrounded her. But better yet, there was a middle ground. She needed to clarify for herself who was *irretrievably* lost—and mourn for them—as well as clarify who was still there for her in relationships that could be challenged, revitalized, and begun anew or restructured. That process became the basis for our couple and family therapy, during which I used the knowledge I had gained over the years about the devastating effects of ambiguous loss.

Studying Ambiguous Loss

The research that enabled me to identify the phenomenon of ambiguous loss was conducted with the families of pilots

declared missing in action in Vietnam and Cambodia. It was   13
1974, and I was collaborating with staff at the Center of
Prisoner of War Studies in the U.S. Naval Health Research
Institute in San Diego. We interviewed the wives of missing
pilots in their homes, and it was from them that I first learned
about the power of ambiguity in complicating loss. I tried to
determine how to ease their stress in spite of the ambiguity
they had to live with—in many cases, for a lifetime. Not only
was there a lack of information, but there was no official
verification that anything had been lost. Interviews with
forty-seven families of MIAs, conducted in California, Hawaii, and Europe, showed that the wife's continuing to keep
her husband psychologically present in the family when he
was physically missing negatively affected both her and her
family. When she kept her MIA husband psychologically
present for emotional support and help in decision-making,
the family exhibited higher conflict and a lower level of
functioning.

In one family, for example, discipline for unruly children
was nonexistent because the mother always said, "Wait until
your dad comes home." In another case, a wife deferred
financial decisions because her husband had always made
them. Overall, a wife's emotional health was improved by
giving up on the search for evidence of her husband's return
and by becoming involved in new relationships. This study,
which showed that the presence of a family member is psychologically, if not physically, measurable, was the first to
demonstrate that ambiguous loss is distressful and leads to
depressive symptoms. It also indicated that neither physical
presence nor physical absence tells the whole story of who is
in and who is out of people's lives, because there is also a

14   psychological family. These findings and those of other studies support the thesis that ambiguous loss is the most difficult loss people face and that absence and presence are psychological as well as physical phenomena in families.

Today, more than two thousand families are still wondering about the whereabouts of their loved ones from the Vietnam war alone. Occasionally, when the political climate allows, bits of human remains trickle home—a tooth or a bone fragment. But even with verification by forensics experts, families never know for sure if the body part actually belongs to their missing family member or if that person is really dead, since such minute fragments could conceivably be taken from living people. Worn out by waiting, however, most families accept what they finally get as theirs to bury. A symbolic closure is better than none at all. Yet others refuse to believe their case is closed and pressure officials here and in Vietnam to keep on looking.

In 1987, to test my theory in more everyday situations of physical loss in families, I surveyed 140 midlife mothers and fathers whose adolescent children had just left home.[3] The families were primarily middle-class Euro-Americans. Leaving home represents in this population a blurred rather than a clear-cut transition, with older teenagers being both in and out of the family. I found that the more strongly these parents perceived their absent adolescent as still present, the more distress the parents experienced. Specifically, thinking a lot about the children, missing them, wondering where they were and what they were doing, hoping for their return home, and having difficulty accepting that they had grown up were closely associated with parental negativity, illness, anxiety, and depression. Although their preoccupation with the loss decreased with time, the fathers reported more depression, insomnia, and somatic symptoms such as backaches, headaches, and stomach ailments than the mothers, suggesting that "the empty nest syndrome" affects fathers even more than mothers. Indeed, the mothers in this study—mostly homemakers or part-time employees—were often pleased that their children had left home, whereas the fathers expressed regret at not having spent more time with their offspring. The fathers, more than the mothers, were psychologically preoccupied with the absent child.

In order to minimize the loss associated with a child's leaving home, parents must change their perceptions of who that child is. Once a son or daughter has grown, the family portrait must be revised. The dependent child is now a young adult, and must be treated as such. Relationships with growing children are excellent examples of the continual challenge parents face to change their perceptions of who's in and who's out of the family. This is especially important during times of transition, such as when children go off to school, get jobs, fall in love, marry, have children of their own, and eventually take care of those who once cared for them.

From 1986 to 1991, I expanded the focus of my research to include families coping with the psychological absence of a loved one. I studied the families of seventy patients with Alzheimer's, almost all of whom were from the Upper Midwest. The severity of the patients' dementia bore no relationship to the extent of their caregivers' depressive symptoms. Rather, it was the degree to which the family caregivers saw the patients as "absent" or "present" that strongly predicted their depressive symptoms, and this connection was even stronger three years after my initial visits with the families.[4]

16   Just as with the MIA research, I found that those with loved
      ones who were "there but not there" were indeed more
      distressed than those who had suffered a more ordinary loss.
          Ambiguous loss from psychological absence is also experi-
      enced by families coping with other chronic mental illnesses,
      such as addiction to drugs or alcohol. The sick family mem-
      ber is present but his or her mind is not. As with dementia,
      family members learn to "walk on eggshells" because they
      never know if their loved one is going to be one way or
      another—like having a Dr. Jekyll and Mr. Hyde in the family.
      To make the situation even more stressful for families experi-
      encing terminal illness, death can now be postponed by tech-
      nology to the point where some families have shed all of their
      tears before the funeral.
          A more subtle but no less real example of a loss that results
      from psychological absence, one that I often see with couples
      in my practice, occurs when one partner is having an affair or,
      even more common today, when one partner is preoccupied
      with work outside the home. The relationship becomes
      threatened by that person's partial presence. Whatever the
      cause, ambiguous loss from psychological absence, like that
      from physical absence, is the culprit causing distress for cou-
      ples and families in diverse situations.

Cultural Differences

As I continued to study both psychological and physical
losses, I began to wonder if my findings and interpretations in
the Alzheimer caregiver studies were ethnocentric. I was curious about how families not as concerned with mastering the
illness would respond to ambiguous loss. So I began meeting

with some Anishinabe women in northern Minnesota who lived in families where an elder had dementia. As we sat in a circle with the sweet smell of burning sage, I listened to their stories. I learned that these Native American women cope with the psychological absence of a demented parent by combining mastery of the situation with a spiritual acceptance of the illness. The Anishinabe women took charge, making sure that their parents saw the right doctors and took their medication, but at the same time, they accepted the challenge that nature had given them. They saw an elderly person's illness as part of nature's cycle from birth to death. One woman said, "I just believe things happen the way they happen because that's the way they're meant to be. And that's what's happening now. Mother's meant to be the way she is and everything that happens bad, I don't care what it is, there's always good comes out of it if you look far enough." Another explained, "We lost the mother that we once knew, but [I] also look at it that she is the child now and I am the mother . . . I had a funeral for Ma because the woman that I knew was just not there anymore." The women's goal of harmony with nature rather than mastery over it, their patience and humor, and their comfort with ambiguity opened up a new path for my thinking. From them I learned that ambiguous loss does not have to devastate.[5]

The Anishinabe women were able to cope with debilitating illness because they believed that life is a mystery that they must embrace and give themselves to willingly. This belief is clearly illustrated in an Anishinabe morning prayer: "I step into the day; I step into myself; I step into the mystery." The women were comfortable with not knowing what lay ahead for their sick loved ones or for themselves as caregivers. But

18   this is not the case with most of my clients. As a family
therapist in a city full of colleges and universities, I most often
see people who are accustomed to having access to information; when they have a problem they want to solve it and
move on. Ambiguity makes them anxious. I do of course
encounter city-dwellers with spiritual beliefs, and they, like
the Anishinabe women on the reservation, tend to remain
resilient despite their experience of ambiguous loss. Although
more research is needed, this suggests that our tolerance for
ambiguity is related to our spiritual beliefs and cultural values, not just to our personality. Whatever the source, such
beliefs and values are helpful in tempering our need to find
definitive solutions when dealing with an illness that won't
get better or a loss that cannot be clarified. Without such
resilience, people faced with situations beyond their control
often break down.

The existence of rituals to mark ambiguous losses is an
indicator of a culture's tolerance for ambiguity. There are few
such markers in the United States. Only recently have greet-
ing cards appeared that express support for people experiencing something as common as the break-up of a relationship.
Only recently have hospitals begun to recognize miscarriage
and infant death as real losses that warrant grieving. In the
past, nonrecognition of newborn loss made sense because
infant mortality rates were so high. In most cultures, mothers
and fathers were encouraged to defer attachment to their
baby until they were sure the child would live. While such
beliefs made sense historically, it is dysfunctional for women
today to be expected to act as if nothing has happened when
they experience a miscarriage or give birth to a stillborn.

In the United States, mainstream assumptions about how

the world works tend to be mastery-oriented. We believe we can master our own destinies because we assume that the world is a fair and logical place where effort matches outcome. Good things happen to good and hard-working people—and conversely, bad things will happen only if we have done something wrong or failed to put in enough effort. This philosophy results in a great deal of stress when people face a problem that cannot be solved, such as an ambiguous loss.

In order to help others cope with such loss, we must first understand their tolerance for the unknown. Family members, neighbors, and therapists must talk together as they try to reach a consensus about how they will respond to the inevitable ambiguities concerning who is in or out of the lives of children and adults who have suffered a loss. This need to communicate is true even within individual couples because each partner may have been socialized with different beliefs and values. Certainly they will have had different experiences. Thus a husband and wife may respond differently when a child is missing. Family members of different genders and generations will often vary in how they interpret an unclear loss. The goal is to achieve some degree of convergence. If couples or family members do not try to understand how they make sense out of the obscurity surrounding their loss, they will be less able to make the decisions necessary for everyday living. Managing family life will become difficult if not impossible.

I remember one couple whose tolerance for the unknown might serve as a lesson for those of us who were socialized to be self-sufficient, masterly, and independent. Their child was dying, and yet they had learned to accept "the deck of cards that was dealt" them. Instead of clinging to the plan they had

22   the outside environment of troubled individuals and distressed families.

Second, I assume that persistent distress is not good for any individual or family, but that in spite of continuing ambiguity, people have the potential to recover and thrive by learning how to *manage* the stress. My approach to teaching family stress management is eclectic and includes psychoeducational, experiential, and structural work. Families are given information, the opportunity to spend time with other families facing similar situations, and guidance on how to reorganize their family. When families of the chronically mentally ill are referred to me, I attempt to help them learn to manage the stress of living with the ambiguity of absence and presence that comes with illnesses such as dementia, schizophrenia, or bipolar disorders. I vividly remember one such family.

Mary was having a manic episode and was so distraught that she had to be hospitalized for her own safety. This was her second hospitalization, and her two teenage daughters were extremely distressed. Before I was to meet with her family, the psychiatrist in charge of her hospitalization wrote me a hurried note: "The expressed emotion in this family is off the wall. The children need to ignore or insulate themselves from some of Mary's symptoms right now if they are to stay okay. They're becoming helpless themselves. They're saying things like I can't take this anymore, and I've been trying to minimize that saying, 'Okay, she went bananas; you've got her in the hospital, things are going okay; she's improving each day. You know, you can live through this, you can survive this.'"

Although the children's distress was understandable, it wasn't doing them or Mary any good. Their stress level had to come down. In the weeks that followed, the girls talked about their mother's (and grandmother's) disorder, what they could do to minimize their chances of getting it, and how they could improve the family's communication patterns. As a group, Mary and her daughters practiced being less critical and more positive, and they discussed the girls' concerns about Mary's not taking her medication and their fear of future episodes. We talked about the daughters' fears of getting the disease that had gripped their mother and grandmother; and we made explicit plans for what to do if their mother—or either of them—became depressed or highly elated in the future. Knowing how to manage the ambiguity of the illness helped ease this family's stress.

The third assumption I make when working with families suffering ambiguous loss is that information should be shared with them, even if that information is "I don't know what the outcome will be." Too often, therapists and physicians assume that only trained professionals can comprehend the technical facts about an illness or event of loss. Research papers are not offered to lay people. Withholding information is patronizing and disrespectful to families, many of whom have loved ones who are able and motivated to read such literature. Clinicians need to realize that by sharing knowledge they are empowering families to take control of their situation even when ambiguity exists.

Fourth, I assume that ambiguous losses can traumatize. In this way, the symptoms of unresolved grief are similar to Post Traumatic Stress Disorder (PTSD). PTSD is a disorder resulting from psychologically stressing events that were outside the realm of usual human experience. These events were never resolved and thus are continually reexperienced, even

24 years after the original event. Ambiguous loss is also a psychologically distressing event that is outside the realm of
ordinary human experience; like the events triggering PTSD,
it lacks resolution and traumatizes. But with ambiguous loss,
the trauma (the ambiguity) continues to exist in the present.
It is not *post* anything. Ambiguous loss is typically a long-
term situation that traumatizes and immobilizes, not a single
event that later has flashback effects.

The outcomes of PTSD are also similar, though not iden-
tical, to outcomes of long-term ambiguous loss. Both can
result in depression, anxiety, psychic numbing, distressing
dreams, and guilt. But ambiguous loss is unique in that
the trauma goes on and on in what families describe as a
rollercoaster ride, during which they alternate between
hope and hopelessness. A loved one is missing, then sighted,
then lost again. Or a family member is dying, then goes
into remission, then the illness returns again in full force.
Hopes are raised and dashed so many times that psychically
people no longer react. Just as animals lay down in their
cages and no longer tried to avoid the pain in early ex-
periments of erratically placed electric shocks, people experiencing trauma out of which they can't make sense feel
helpless and no longer act.

Although the focus on family stress management does not
exclude the possibility of individual and group therapies, my
approach centers on encouraging couples and families to
talk together, sharing information as well as their perceptions and feelings, and eventually come to a consensus on
how to celebrate the part of their loved one that is still
present and mourn the part that is lost. By telling their story
to someone who will listen and help make sense of it,

families receive the validation they need to move forward with the grieving process. No matter what their beliefs, values, or theoretical preferences, with the right kind of intervention, people can learn to live well despite suffering ambiguous loss.

⤜ 2 ⤛

Leaving without Goodbye

The absent are always present.
Carol Shields, *The Stone Diaries*

IT WAS AN EARLY SPRING DAY IN WASHINGTON, D.C., WHEN
I visited the Vietnam War Memorial and found myself surrounded by a quiet crowd of schoolchildren, tourists, and still
grieving relatives. Of special interest to me were the names of
the missing soldiers, or MIAs. Unlike prisoners of war, who
eventually came home or were found dead, these men are still
lost. Their families, not knowing if they are dead or alive,
endure a special kind of agony. As I walked in silence past the
endless names, I noticed a blue hair ribbon, a pack of Camels,
and a hand-written note on the ground below the name of a
man still missing. "There will never be a day when I won't
think of you," the note read.

Most people need the concrete experience of seeing the
body of a loved one who has died because it makes loss real.
Most families of missing persons never find such verification
of death and thus face greater challenges in shifting their
perceptions about absence or presence. For relatives of those

soldiers whose names are engraved as "MIA," even the Vietnam Memorial cannot bring certainty of death.

The families of missing soldiers that I studied had difficulty finding closure because the uncertainty was extreme and persistent. With frustrating regularity, there were just enough reports claiming that some of the men were still alive to rekindle a grief that was beginning to heal. Families could not complete their mourning when their loss remained so uncertain. My research showed that wives of these missing men kept their families functioning, but often at their own emotional expense. I was particularly interested in the wives' *perceptions* of the ambiguity surrounding their loss. How did they make sense of it? How did they cope and move on in spite of it?

In California, I interviewed the wife of a missing pilot several years after her husband's plane had been shot down over southeast Asia. We had just completed a long questionnaire, and I was about ready to leave when she told me a story I will never forget. She was seeing me to the door, and I almost didn't tune into what she was saying because I thought I had all the information I needed. She told me her husband had come back to talk with her twice since he was shot down. The first time he came to visit her they had a conversation in the driveway in front of their house. He told her to sell the house, get a bigger one to accommodate their four growing children, and move to a better school district. She said he also told her to sell the car and get a station wagon to make room for the soon-to-be teenagers and their things. Though she had never made such decisions before, she now did everything he told her to do. About a year later, she said, her husband returned for a second visit. This time their conversation took place in the bedroom. He told her she had done a good job, that he was

28 proud of her and loved her, and that he was now going to say goodbye. "This is when I knew he was really dead," she said.

I found this woman's story eye-opening not only because of what she was saying but because of the intensity of her conviction that these visits had really happened. I had been trained as a social scientist to record only objective data, objective reality. Yet, to paraphrase the symbolic interactionist W. I. Thomas, because this woman perceived her story to be true, it was true in its consequences.[1] Conversations with her missing husband comforted and reassured her, enabling her to make necessary decisions and changes that she might not otherwise have been able to make. His symbolic presence provided direction and, importantly, the time she needed to adapt to her new role as a single parent and head of the family.

Some time later, this woman told me that she had grown up on an Indian reservation where it was the custom, in the case of sudden death, to keep the deceased person "present" for a while to ease the abruptness of the loss. Her eagerness for her MIA husband's symbolic presence was an important lesson. Although her story did not fit my requirements at that time for "hard" data, I could see that her experience was *real to her* and had benefited her functioning and, consequently, her children's well-being. Her story forever changed the way I think about and do research.

While this wife of a missing pilot found a way to adapt to her family's ambiguous loss, many people do not. Their grief remains unresolved and they cannot move on. Sometimes whole societies are affected by such a loss. In 1958 Imre Nagy, the beloved prime minister of Hungary, disappeared. The rumor was that he had been shot, but officially this was denied—and there was no grave. Not until 1989 was Nagy's body produced and a public funeral held in his honor. People came for a massive display of grief that finally brought closure to a nation's ambiguous loss.

Even on a national level, healing requires some measure of clarity. Only when things are made right again—bodies produced, services held, and grieving validated by the larger community—can people put their losses to rest. But often the evidence verifying death is grim. From 1975 to 1979, until the Khmer Rouge regime of Pol Pot was driven from power, more than fourteen thousand Cambodian prisoners were detained, tortured, and killed. Like the Nazis, the Khmer Rouge kept a death list, but theirs included photographs.[2] Today relatives of missing family members can find certainty in this macabre record, entitled *The Killing Fields,* where portraits taken of frightened people just before their execution are the only certification of their death. Such records may be of some help to families because they give assurance of death, but like Nazi records of Holocaust victims, they do not lessen the horror.

Mysterious disappearances are always a consequence of war and political conflict. Native Americans, Jews, Russians, Hmong, Cambodians, Tibetans, Bosnians, and Rwandans all share a history of traumatic uprooting and near annihilation. During the Rwandan conflict, a health care worker, Emeritha Uwizeyimana, was separated from her husband and children. After two and a half years as a refugee, she found her children but her anxiety continued: "I wait for news of my husband. I just want to know if he's dead or alive."[3] Such stories are not unusual, and the lack of a goodbye to those who mysteriously disappeared continues to haunt survivors and subsequent generations.

The American legacy of ambiguous loss also has a trau-

30   matic social history—the uprooting of Africans who were brought by force to the shores of the United States and sold off with little concern for preserving marriages and families. In Alex Haley's *Roots*, we see the endless struggle of a husband and wife and their children to stay together—in mind if not in body. Given this history of resilience in the face of traumatic ambiguous losses, it is no wonder that contemporary African American families define family with less rigid boundaries than those with European roots.

When working with people experiencing unresolved losses, family therapists and researchers must not label as pathological their resistance to forming new attachments and restructuring the family. Their adaptations may be dysfunctional, but that is not the same as saying that the person or family is dysfunctional. In the absence of clarity, people understandably cling to the status quo, because at some level they hope that the person who is missing will some day return. Even community, church, and medical professionals often inadvertently contribute to the stagnation of grief because they are not accustomed to giving support unless there is a certified loss. When such clarity is lacking, families are on their own. As with the wife of the missing pilot, people must find their own way out of the ambiguity.

Many unclear goodbyes in everyday family life also fall outside the traditional categories of loss but nonetheless cause distress. Frequent among them are the absences associated with divorce, adoption, migration, and overcommitment to work.

Divorce, for example, provides a fertile ground for confusion about the absence or presence of a noncustodial parent.

The family portrait, a well-known symbol of who is in and who is out of a family, often documents the confusion within the family following divorce and remarriage. Professional photographers are increasingly asked to delete a divorced mate from family photographs, only to be asked by the offspring years later to put the absent parent back in again. Wedding photographers now take twice as many photos at weddings because the bride and groom often ask for separate posings with their divorced parents and the parents' new mates.

The family event of divorce, now all too common, can be better understood and managed by everyone involved if it is viewed as an ambiguous loss. Something was lost but something is still there; the marriage is lost, but the parenting continues (one would hope that grandparenting on both sides would continue as well). Identifying what has been lost and grieving it while also identifying the connections that continue in their lives is a healthier approach for children than simply saying, "Mommy and Daddy don't love each other any more, but they will always love you." Children often have trouble trusting this statement. They know they have lost something; we might as well validate that for them as we stress what remains the same in their family. In addition, children and adults are relieved to learn that what they are experiencing has a name. The trouble is not divorce per se—indeed, for many families divorce has no deleterious effects—but the ambiguity and unresolved loss that often accompany it. The loss associated with divorce is often more difficult than the loss that results from death because the former remains inherently unclear. The idea of ambiguous loss provides children and adults with a way to comprehend their situation and learn to live more functionally with divorce.

In my own case, I initially rejected family therapist Carl Whitaker's pronouncement, "You can never get divorced!" But years later, when my former husband and I cohosted a dinner for our son's wedding, when he called to tell me of a mutual friend's death, and when he and I took our new spouses to our daughter's holiday dinner parties and birthday celebrations for our grandchildren, I realized Whitaker was right. Old relationships do not simply disappear; they continue for most of us even in a revised family portrait.

Learning to live with the ambiguity of divorce and remarriage requires a whole new set of skills. The first is to revise our perception of who our family is and who it is not. To determine this we might ask ourselves whom we would invite to a special family celebration or ritual such as a wedding, graduation, bar mitzvah, baptism, or birthday. Such guest lists quickly reveal whom we consider "family" or "coparent" as well as whom we exclude as family. Today, the lists often include divorced partners and their new mates.

All this requires a second skill, the ability to let go of needing an absolute and precise definition of family. This is not easy because the beliefs and values associated with the family will vary immensely among people and regions. It helps to recognize that we are already more flexible than we think, taking in a sister's child, letting go of adult children as they grow up, cooperating as parents even after a divorce, or taking care of grandchildren. Rather than weakening the family, such elasticity in family composition enhances resilience and flexibility. Finally, this process of continuity and change requires periodic rethinking of who is part of the family, particularly during times of transition, such as when people enter the family through marriage, remarriage, or birth and exit through separation, divorce, or death. The ambiguous entries and exits associated with remarriage and divorce will always cause stress.

In a sense one has to abandon the concept of monogamy in order to make divorce and remarriage work because a first marriage does not simply stop when a second one starts. It is forever a part of the fabric of one's life. As with a death certificate, a divorce decree cannot erase the experience, good or bad; consequently, often more than a memory remains in subsequent relationships. And with divorce, unlike death, the ex-mate is often physically present, especially if there are children to coparent. Being able to live with the ambiguity inherent in such situations is one of the main secrets to a successful remarriage.

In my clinical work I saw Debra, who had been divorced from John for more than two years but was unable to make a new life for herself because she still felt married and con-trolled. "My husband divorced me," she said, "but he keeps coming back into my life. When he picks up or returns the children, he wants to come in and talk. He even asks for a cup of coffee—or worse yet, opens the cupboard and helps him-self. Even the kids think it's strange. It's driving me crazy! How can I forget him when he keeps coming back?"

"You can't," I said. "You had three children and a twenty-year relationship with him. You can't forget that, nor should you. But you can revise the relationship." We talked about setting boundaries for the marital relationship that was over while keeping the parental relationship going. Not needing to close John entirely out of her life eased Debra's tension. She

34   wanted him involved with their children; he was a good
father and she needed his help. But it took her a while longer
to identify how to disconnect from the marriage. Unaccustomed to setting boundaries with John in a house they had
shared for so long, she had difficulty keeping him out of what
was now *her* house and *her* cupboards. Over time, various
people came with Debra to her sessions with me—her mom,
her sisters, her ex-husband and his current wife (who came
along mostly as a listener and I suspect to make sure that I
wasn't aiming for a reconciliation). In the end, Debra came to
define herself and her family more clearly. Among other
things, she told John not to come into the house unless he was
invited. He seemed miffed, but I could see that his present
wife eagerly supported this idea and readily soothed his cha-
grin. Debra seemed pleased as well. John was not entirely out
of her life, but she was clearer now about when he was in and
when he was out, what was over and what continued. It is
this kind of redrawing of the family in situations of divorce
and remarriage that makes possible a greater chance for
peace and harmony. Divorced families do not have to be
"broken families"; they can simply be reconstructed versions
of the original. When the marriage contract is dissolved, not
everything is lost.

    Some people, however, can't tolerate the ambiguity of who
is in or out of their families after divorce. For those who can't,
there are superficial "solutions." As mentioned, enterprising
photographic technicians can now change people's marital
history by "rubbing out" those who are no longer wanted in
a wedding or family photograph. Many are apparently so
discomforted by the old portraits that they are willing to pay
high prices for their revision.

This same discomfort with ambiguity is addressed by members of divorced families who stay connected. The family is still a family, but it has a different structure now. If, for example, a portrait of the "old" family is absolutely necessary for children, why not encourage them to construct a collage of all those people they consider family? This would be more honest than the artificial posing of people who are uncomfortable being together in the same room. Photographs—even a collage—are just symbols, however; eventually family members must change their perceptions about who constitutes the family. Even so, if relatives want to stay in touch individually with those who used to be in their official family, why not? Their view of family may not seem real to others, but it is real for them.

Loss without closure may also occur in the everyday situation of adoption. Although the birth mother is more conscious of the actual separation than is the baby given up for adoption, both can be affected by ambiguous loss. The child, too, may wonder where the mother is, if she is well, or what she is like.

One way to determine adoptive parents' tolerance for ambiguity may be to explore whether they chose an open or closed adoption. When adoption files are voluntarily open and all parties are known to one another, the adopting family appears to be able to tolerate ambiguity and is able to think about, even include, the birth mother in their lives. In closed adoptions, where files are locked, adoptive parents appear to prefer the absolute of no contact. Regardless of the type of adoption chosen, however, researchers are finding that the birth mother is thought about often and kept psychologically present in the minds of *both* the adopted mother and the

36   adopted child.[4] The psychological family is a reality for those affected by adoption, too.

In my own practice I have worked with adopted people troubled by the ambiguity of not knowing the identity or whereabouts of their biological parents. Their need to know is often strongest when they begin thinking about starting their own families. With a more flexible view of family, their search to solve this mystery does not have to erode their relationship with their adoptive parents. Even when biological parents are found, the adoptive parents remain the *real* parents, for as many adopted kids will say, "they were there for me in the middle of the night." Physical presence even more than genetics defines a parent in a child's eyes. A few adoptees have told me that, in retrospect, not knowing might have been better, but many continue to take the risk of searching for their biological roots. For them, knowing is necessary to resolve the loss, even if their search yields news that is less than ideal.

Acting as if the membership list of an adoptive family is etched in stone may in the end be more stressful than explicitly recognizing that the family has ambiguous boundaries—some people in all the time, some in some of the time, and some out all the time. A clear fluidity, as opposed to an unspoken ambiguity, is not harmful in adoptive family relationships if it is openly recognized by everyone, including the children.

Perhaps the most common break in one's perception of family comes from immigration. A wave of immigration from Continental Europe and Ireland occurred a century ago, peaking in 1909 with 1.2 million immigrants passing through the gates of Ellis Island into the United States that year alone. Today, America remains a nation of immigrants, though now the points of departure are most often Mexico, Latin America, and Asia. With fewer restrictions on travel, people worldwide are on the move. Even within the United States families continue to move around, from countryside to city, from East to West, from North to South, and then back again. In a world where people are constantly uprooting, the legacy of ambiguous loss remains strong.

My own family and many others in the American Midwest share this legacy from the massive immigration movement that stretched from the middle 1800s to the turn of the last century. Norwegian, German, Finnish, Irish, and Swiss families emigrated to settle here. Leaving Europe was traumatic, for it was unlikely they would ever return. Farewells were especially difficult for the women. Just as their families began to take root in America and they began to feel settled, historical diaries tell us that many of their husbands insisted on going even farther west into the Dakotas or to the flats of Nebraska or California, usually for more land or for gold. As the men followed their itch for adventure, the uprooting and repeated goodbyes took a high toll on immigrant women on the plains whose family connections had already been broken.

Hamlin Garland in his stories about the middle border between the Midwest and the frontier farther west, wrote of watching his mother reluctantly uproot once again because his father yearned to move west: "One by one the women put their worn, ungraceful arms about her, kissed her with trembling lips, and went away in silent grief. The scene became too painful for me at last, and I fled away from it—out into the fields, bitterly asking, 'Why should this suffering be? Why

38 should mother be wrenched from all her dearest friends and forced to move away to a strange land?'"[5]

Garland describes how, at family holidays, his father and the other men always wanted to sing a song his mother and the other women disliked. It went: "Cheer up, brothers, as we go, / O'er the mountain, westward ho." Garland describes the scene: "My father's face shone with the light of the explorer, the pioneer. The words appealed to him as the finest poetry. It meant all that was fine and hopeful and buoyant in American life to him—but on my mother's sweet face, a wistful expression deepened and in her fine eyes a shadow lay. To her, this song meant not so much the acquisition of a new home as the loss of all her friends and relatives . . . that song meant deprivation, suffering, loneliness, heartache."[6]

For many immigrant women on the midwestern frontier, the repetition of traumatic goodbyes became too much and they simply gave up. Historical documents from the old asylum in St. Peter, Minnesota, verify that this institution became a haven for some women who could not face yet one more uprooting.[7]

Even when midwestern immigrant women were able to settle in one place, their broken connections with family back home were painful. Loneliness engulfed them. They particularly missed their mothers and sisters in times of childbirth or illness. A Wisconsin journalist who recorded oral histories writes:

> One family recounts how the father and mother both fell ill with cholera during the epidemic [of 1853]. The wife was so weak that she was unable to walk and the husband was unable to get out of bed, yet was burning up with fever. He told his wife that if he could have a drink of water, he thought he could get well.

Their house was between three quarters and a mile from the Sugar River from which their water was obtained. There was no one to get the water so the wife took a small bucket, placed the handle in her teeth, and painfully and slowly crawled the distance to the stream, pushing her way through tall grass, woods, and underbrush. She dipped the pail into the water and carried it back in the same manner. Her husband lived.[8]

There were few people to help such women with their caregiving duties. Neighbors were too far away; kinfolk were back in the old country. Physically cut off from mothers and sisters who ordinarily would have been there for them, these immigrant women endured a painful isolation that was outside the realm of ordinary human experience.

The unclear goodbyes of immigration also affected the mothers left behind as their daughters and sons departed for the United States. Anna—a woman I often saw working in her garden as I walked to school as a teenager—kept letters she received from her mother back in Switzerland. They illustrate the sadness of knowing she would never again see her daughter and sons, who were always on her mind. On December 2, 1926, Anna's mother wrote this letter:

> Dear Anna,
> Thank you for the money and the beautiful family picture you sent us. All of your children look so pretty in their nice clothes. But you, dear Anna, you look so thin. One can see that you have gone through a lot . . . I can't look at your picture long enough, even though I cry each time I do. I am so lonesome for you, Ambrose, and Carl in America. I know that I will never see any of you in this world again.[9]

The Irish may have been more direct in facing their unclear goodbyes. When their children left for America, parents actu-

40 ally thought of such departures as funerals. In this way, the community-sanctioned farewell ritual may have helped families find closure by symbolically finalizing the goodbye; they knew full well they might never see their children again. An old manuscript tells the story: "It was just like a big funeral . . . and the last parting . . . was indeed sad to see . . . The parents especially were so sad, as if the person leaving were really dead . . . You would rather not be there at all if you would be any way soft yourself."[10]

Such ambiguous losses continued to cause distress during the massive emigrations a century ago across the Atlantic to the United States. While listening to oral histories at Ellis Island, I heard that same pain described by a Swiss-Bernese woman who, as a girl, had seen her father leave for America while she, her siblings, and her mother had to stay behind: "I can still see me and my brother and sister; we're standing there waving. My mother is crying and it's one of those things—it's like a photographic thing that stays with you. We were crying, too. By the way my mother talked, she was so afraid that he would never come back. That he would be swallowed up in the ocean—because it was so far away. And this is what her feeling was—that she would never see him again."[11]

My paternal grandmother, Sophie Grossenbacher, was a mother left behind. Her many letters reveal the life-long ambiguity she experienced as a result of being emotionally close to my father yet physically separated from him. She would always begin with "My dears" and end with: "May God protect you always. Mother." She wrote a letter just about every month, often ending with: "It is a big pleasure for me to chat with you a little. If only today I could be with you." But then World War II began, and the bombs came dangerously

close to her home on the Swiss border, near Basel. She wrote:
"My dears: Finally a few lines from me. I had the blues bad today. I would say I was longing for my dear ones far away." She wrote of hard economic times and the fear of war, ending with: "I think of you every day. You have two big girls now [my sister and me]. I wish I could see them."

In 1943, when mail was sporadic owing to the war, she wonders if her letters have gotten through and longs for word from her son in America: "How are you doing over there? I hope all is well. I am asked by all your brothers and sisters if I have any news from you. Yes, we are all longing for a letter from you and to find out how you are doing. After such a long silence, we are longing to hear from you. Even if it is not possible to write, I am with you at all times anyway in my thoughts. I am sure you have two big sons by now [my brothers]. I wish I could see them in person. Many times, I take the pictures out of the drawer just to look at them. Write as soon as you can."

After the war, letters were exchanged more regularly. "How you make us all so happy with your letters, which we all like to read . . . Even though I cannot do anything for you anymore, I think of you every day, and I pray for you that you all will stay well and healthy. I will now close my chat. Don't look at my mistakes. I feel that my thoughts are getting too weak to write letters [Sophie is now seventy-nine years old]."

After the war it became possible to make a transatlantic phone call, so for her eightieth birthday, my father placed his first and only call to his mother. I recall the event vividly. My sister and I were able to say "Salut, Grossmuetti" ("Hello, Grandmother"). Those were the only words I ever spoke to her, and it was the only time I was ever to hear her voice.

42   It took a long time for my grandmother to write after that phone call because her health was failing:

> I want to thank you for the great happiness you caused me on my birthday. Yes, Paul, the feeling it gave me when I could hear your voice, it cannot be described in words. I felt like you were standing among us when I could hear you talk. And how the "Salut, Grossmuetti" from your two daughters made me happy. I even heard them laugh. And then your wife, Vereneli, came on the phone. I was hoping that we could chat for a longer time because it was so chummy. I can tell you that it was an important moment for us all. All your dear ones here got up from the table [and came] to the telephone to hear your voice, if only for a word or two. That day, we will always remember. And we all hope that for our next family get-together, you will be in our midst. I hope it is soon, because for me, one cannot know when the last day will come.[12]

That letter was written in 1945. My father, strapped with work and farm debt, still could not return. In 1948 his mother wrote: "I would like to hear your music and songs and be among you all. I will be there in my thoughts. Fritz in Basel told me that you have too much work and you cannot come home yet. I understand that a farm like yours requires a lot of work. I would have liked to see you, but I will endure and still hope for a reunion."

Finally, in the fall of 1949, when her health worsened, my father booked passage on a ship to Europe. He knew his mother was holding on until she could see him once more. There was only enough money for one passage, so he went alone while my mother ran the farm and household. My father's visit to Switzerland lasted six weeks. His mother said her wish had come true and that now she was content to die.

A few months later, she died. But just before she did, one last letter arrived for my father—this time written by a grandchild in the household: "Your letter made her really happy. She is really glad that all of you are well. She sends her best wishes."

The announcement of Sophie Grossenbacher's death arrived, as is the Swiss custom, in an envelope bordered in black. My father knew what it was without opening it and his grief was deep. As with many immigrants, his mourning was complicated because he could not be with his family back home for the funeral and burial or for the communal grieving and remembering. Cut off from all of the mourning rituals, he felt isolated and alone. I remember that although we tried, we were of little comfort because we had never really been an active part of his mother's life except for that one phone call.

Our desire for freedom of mobility and perhaps adventure—or our economic need—may explain why ambiguous losses are common even today. Uncertain goodbyes associated with uprooting are piled on top of other ambiguous losses caused by expected transitions—kids growing up and leaving home and parents growing older and frail—as well as unexpected losses resulting from divorce, captivity, or disappearance. Such partial losses will powerfully affect our lives. We can succumb to them or, like the wife of the missing pilot, overcome them and move on. Or we can adapt and endure, as Sophie Grossenbacher did.

Our ability to overcome ambiguous loss from immigration is influenced by our personal and cultural legacy. According to Salman Akhtar, a psychiatrist and analyst from Philadelphia, many factors can influence the psychological outcomes

44   of immigration.[13] Among those that affect immigrants' adaptation to their new home are the permanence of the move, whether they moved of their own volition, the possibility of returning home to visit, age, optimism, reception in their new land, and the similarity between their role in the new country and their role in their homeland. Underlying such factors is the ability to stay connected to the old country while putting down roots in the new.

Whatever the cause of unresolved loss—immigration, war, divorce, remarriage, or adoption—its symptoms can be distressing. Anxiety, depression, somatic illnesses, and family conflict often afflict those who do not adapt and move on with their lives. Without some kind of closure, the absent stay present.

⤳ 3 ⤴

Goodbye without Leaving

The Alzheimer's face indicates only an absence. It is, in the
most literal sense, a mask.

John Bayley, "Elegy for Iris," *New Yorker* (July 27, 1998)

PSYCHOLOGICAL ABSENCE CAN BE AS DEVASTATING AS
physical absence. In this type of ambiguous loss, a loved one is
present, but his or her mind is not. Brain injury, stroke, and
Alzheimer's disease are the prime culprits. Alzheimer's in particular is all too common, affecting one in three families in the
United States. The filmmaker Meirendorf said it succinctly:
"Alzheimer's disease victims never recover and never stop getting worse. They cling to the barest threads of who they once
were: a teacher tries to work a child's puzzle; a craftsman plays
with toys that remind him of his tools. All achievements are
forgotten and faces of loved ones lost. There are endless days
before death comes. Alzheimer's may be the cruelest disease."[1] Indeed, it is cruel to the patients, but it is also cruel to
their families. With Alzheimer's, the more uncertain a family
member is about the patient's status as absent or present, the
greater the family member's symptoms of depression.[2]

46   In my research with Alzheimer's patients, I focused on the experience of families living with the disease. I asked them to describe especially stressful events. The family members were surprised; they were used to being asked only about how the patient was doing. I learned, too, from my colleagues. Ann, a family therapist and the daughter of an Alzheimer's patient, told me about the pain she experienced when she realized that her mother no longer knew her.

Ann had moved her mother to a nursing home because of the seriousness of her dementia. She visited often even though it was an hour's drive each way. One day when she arrived at the nursing home, she noticed that her mother was calling every blonde woman on the floor "Ann," as though they were all her daughter. Ann was devastated. "Mother doesn't know me anymore. Why do I keep coming to see her?" Ann came to the realization that she was coming for herself. "Sometimes I just lay my head in her lap and guide her hand over my hair, like she used to do."

The poignancy of this scene reminds me of a documentary featuring life with Wes, another Alzheimer's patient, and his wife, Lynn. Wes was diagnosed with the disease in his forties, as were his father and sister. In tests at the veterans' hospital, Wes didn't know the year or the president's name. When asked what day it was, he answered, "About noon, I think." Wes had been a navy pilot. After military service, he became a pioneer in commuter aviation, a community leader, and a successful businessman. Now, in the garden next to his house, he gets turned around and confused about where he is.

Wes's son, Omer, came home from college when his father was diagnosed. "Alzheimer's took from him his life, what he loved, his airport, robbed him of his family, stripped him of all he had and all he spent his life building," Omer explains. "He was a good dad; he had really high standards, taught us never to lie, cheat, steal . . . I respected him for what he was and who he was. He bent over backwards to help us kids. He always tried to do the very best for us . . . Dad was an avid sportsman . . . I never went through a rebellious stage where I hated my father. I really liked him a lot and I always have and still do." But then Omer shifts and speaks of what is gone: "You can't relate with him. Physically he's there but mentally he's not. And as far as I'm concerned, he's not my father. My father died about five or six years ago."

Lynn shares the loss. "It's hard watching [my husband] not being able to do things. He can't accomplish anything." She gives Wes menial tasks to do while she's in the kitchen, but even drying the dishes is a challenge for him. When her husband leaves the room, Lynn is pensive. Hesitatingly, she speaks: "I sometimes—every once in a while, I will look or think—you're leaving me. And I don't want you to go!" [Pause] "But you can't dwell on that either, or you'd just be upset all the time. So you just have your joy in being with him."

Later she brings her husband back into the room. "Do you remember what day it is today?" she asks. "Ummmm, no," he says flatly. "Today is our anniversary." Patting the sofa as if asking him to sit down beside her, she continues, "I got a card from Omer and Kim." She pauses and then reads, "May your anniversary be a day to remember all the fun times filled with laughter, the sentimental times warmed by love." Her voice breaks. She looks up at her ill husband and says softly, "We've been married thirty years today." He laughs and says,

48   "Wow!" She puts her arm around him and says, "I love you." Her embrace is not returned; he just giggles and repeats, "I love you, too."[3]

Ann, Lynn, and Omer lived in that gray zone of ambiguity where someone they loved was gradually slipping away. Della was having a similar experience, but in her case, the dementia was accompanied by violence. She and her husband lived on an isolated farm in North Dakota where she had become accustomed to solving her own problems. But her husband gave her so much trouble that she finally had to ask the county's Alzheimer's support group for help. "He is always mad now and I never know why," she said when I met her at a meeting. "One night—it was thirty below zero—he just up and walked out of the house. Out in the yard, he yelled back at me, 'I'm just going to say goodbye to you here.' He turned around and never looked back." Knowing he could quickly freeze to death on such a night, she ran to the phone to call the sheriff and her brother for help. They found him just in time.

"He wanders a lot," she said at the meeting. "The neighbor women and I chase him out in the cornfields a lot now. But then I get to worrying—if I go out into the cornfield and fall down, then what?" Everyone there was asking the same question.

Della explained that this stage of her husband's illness—when he was still able to walk and was still stronger than she was—was the most difficult for her. "Once he did a half nelson on me. It really hurt. But then I relaxed and he did, too, and let me out of his grip." The group was relieved to hear that Della's husband was no longer violent, but they still worried about her being alone with him.

The difficulties that Ann, Lynn, Omer, and Della were experiencing also distressed Lydia and her family. I was interviewing a three-generation Jewish family in which the elderly grandfather, I'll call him Sol, had advanced Alzheimer's disease. The family was in conflict because Sol's wife, Lydia, who was over seventy, was about to move her husband to a nursing home and go to Florida for a rest with her sister. Most of the adult children in the family thought things should stay as they always had been—Mom should keep Dad at home and continue to care for him there. But the elderly wife and her sister—and, surprisingly, a teenage grandchild—recognized that the unending work was getting to be too much for Lydia. They alone were ready for change. The three generations talked back and forth for several hours, during which I planted the idea that it's all right for family members experiencing ambiguous loss to have differing views of a loved one's absence or presence. The family simply needed to talk together, as they were doing now, to hear one another's perceptions. It was nearing noon, and someone came in from the kitchen to offer food. A strong voice boomed from the back of the room, where the patient's elderly brother had been sitting quietly: "There will be no sitting shiva here! My brother is still alive!" With that, the group dispersed. But I was pleased. Together, the family had clarified some of the ambiguity. Sol was still there. Lydia proceeded with her plans to move him to a home, then took a much-needed vacation with her sister. While she was gone, her children and grandchildren took turns visiting Sol. And thanks to Uncle Jake, everyone was clear that no death had occurred.

Religious rituals for mourning loss are reserved for the clearly dead. There are few ceremonies to comfort us when

50   our loved ones are only partially gone. Families are left on their own to figure out how to cope. In a culture that stresses problem solving, an impending death may be interpreted as failure. Yet it is expected that family members will continue to care for an ambiguously lost loved one to the end. The question of who determines "the end," however, is not always clear, especially when heroic measures conflict with living wills or ambivalent family members.

Few people, professionals or family members, can tolerate for long being in a situation that is out of their control. The stress is too much. As the ambiguity persists, conflicts increase, not just among family members, but also between the family and clinicians. Indeed, even health care workers are not always sure how to respond to families struggling to cope with an ambiguous loss. This is where communication is so important; even telling a family "I don't know what will happen" in response to their questions about the future is more welcome than silence. If families are to care for their chronically ill loved ones when there are few answers, they need help sorting through the emotions that accompany caregiving work in the context of ambiguity. They need to know what effects unresolved grief has on family members. In my clinical practice, I often see clients who present with depression and relationship troubles, but when they call for an appointment, they rarely mention loss and ambiguity. Helen's case is typical. She called about feelings of sadness and hopelessness that wouldn't go away. They were interfering with her work as a surgeon. She had felt this way since her mate of ten years—who was also a partner in her practice—left her the year before. Near the end of the first session, I asked, "Can you think about the other losses you have experienced in your life—the big ones that you still remember?" "Why do they matter now?" she wanted to know. "Maybe they don't," I answered.

Helen returned a week later with a list of her losses. She began deliberately at first, as if reading a grocery list: "One: A major break-up while in medical school. My mate brought a lover home. I had to throw them both out. It was a big loss for me since I cared and thought my mate did, too. Two: My mother has Alzheimer's disease; it's been five years since she last knew me. Three: I lost some good friends after long illnesses to AIDS. Four: My brother. He and I no longer talk—he drinks too much. We were close once but he is no longer the sweet kid I once knew. Five [her voice changes and slows]: My love of ten years who opened my heart."

Helen was quiet. It seemed that she, too, was surprised by the length and crescendo of her list. Then she asked why only the last loss "brought me down." We talked about the proverbial "straw that breaks the camel's back" and the idea that unresolved losses can pile up. I suggested, "In order to heal from that last loss, you may have to revisit those that came before. They are all part of your experience."

We talked about loss and ambiguity and how they mix together and make it difficult for a person to move on. Helen had not thought about it that way before. No one on her list had left with a clean break; all had slipped away gradually. With such an accumulation of ambiguous losses (she had never heard the term before), it was no wonder that her feelings of rejection were mingled with feelings of powerlessness. As a surgeon, Helen was accustomed to being in charge of the situation at hand; the ambiguous losses she suffered caused feelings of helplessness as well as hopelessness.

challenge for all of us. Don [the oldest brother] especially has committed himself to the project. My time with Mom is full of dancing, laughing, ball playing, eating, and joking around. I am finding myself the recipient of complete, unconditional love that is as sweet as honey. I don't know how long this will all last. I'm not sure how she will change. But for now I feel I am in the presence of an illuminated being who is my mom.[4]

This family, perhaps because of their creativity, did not resist change for long. Instead, they enjoyed their mother's new way of being and learned from it. They were delighted when she summed up her situation one morning by declaring, "I am not fictional."[5]

The Sewell family's approach to ambiguous loss was unique in that the brothers came to see their mother as still present, even psychologically. They simply heard her words now as a special language and saw her childlike actions as charming. Even in dementia, her words made sense on some level: "I'm off the mat," or "Clouds are coming, they're forgetting things." Her son Tom heard her words as a kind of avant-garde poetry:

TOM: What do you think when you look at me?
MOM: I love you . . . real big. You may have 3 or 6, I don't know.
TOM: 3 or 6 what?
MOM: Peace, I don't know.

MOM: What's your number, dear?
TOM: You mean my name?
MOM: Yes. What do I call you?
TOM: Tom.

MOM: Where's Dad [her husband]?
TOM: He died about 5 years ago.

MOM: Oh, he didn't continue?

MOM: I'm glad that we met Dad before he died.

MOM: Who are you?
TOM: I'm Tom. Who are you?
MOM: Nothing?
TOM: Nothing?
MOM: There's nothing here. I thought I was but I'm not.

MOM: Don't you ever kiss your mom and your young daughter at night? Then I want some of that right now.

MOM: Oh, Mister, can you help me? If you could I'd tell my mother, my father, and my children that [it's] me. Smart was smart.

MOM [talking about her parents]: Why did they leave us? We're just kids.

MOM: I think they took the stuff and went.
TOM: Who?
MOM: Father and Mother [her parents].

When I was in this home, observing these men tend to their mother, I thought of Rilke: ". . . be patient toward all that is unsolved in your heart and try to love *the questions themselves* like locked rooms and like books that are written in a very foreign tongue . . . And the point is, to live everything. *Live* the questions now. Perhaps you will then gradually, without noticing it, live along some day into the answer."[6]

Ruth was indeed in some locked room and was speaking in a foreign tongue, but her sons embraced the questions—and the lack of answers. They were not immobilized by their mother's mental condition. I recall being invited to their house for a party one holiday season. I arrived late, and the

56   party was in full swing. I went upstairs with my coat and was shocked to see Ruth's bedroom empty. Had she died, I wondered? I came downstairs cautiously, wondering what to say. But to my surprise, there she was in the living room, dressed in sequins, surrounded by a bevy of artistic friends and neighbors, all singing and laughing. When Ruth's glass of egg nog would tip precariously, someone would just reach over and straighten it for her. People talked to her and she to them; no one seemed to mind that her words were incoherent. I thought of all the parties I had gone to where the conversation was just as nonsensical and no one was suffering from Alzheimer's.

My research goal has always been to learn how to lower the stress level of those who must care for family members who are gone but still here. The Sewell family, as much as any formal research, showed me a more positive way for both patient and family to live with ambiguous loss. They ignored convention by continuing the joyous part of their lives together; they did not talk of tragedy. Perhaps their artistic sensibilities helped them to adjust to the change in their family. They did not see their mother as "gone": they simply learned to shift their view day to day, depending on what her illness brought. They were even able to enjoy her new way of being. To be sure, not all Alzheimer's patients are so cheerful, but the Sewells' extraordinary resilience and creativity can serve as an inspiration for all those confronting such a loss.

Ambiguous loss results not only from chronic mental illnesses but also from unclear goodbyes in daily life. An all-too-ordinary example is the preoccupation with work. When people we care about are continually obsessed with their work, they are not really "there" for us.

After working with his wife, Marge, in couple's therapy, Phil began coming home earlier, thinking this would fix his wife's complaint that he was gone so much. But it did not. The tension continued. As Marge put it, he was still "at the office. His head is always in his briefcase!" Phil agreed: "I'm home, but I feel like I still have something around me, like Saran Wrap. I'm still at work even when I'm home."

Phil was physically present but psychologically absent. He might just as well have stayed at the office, for his unavailability was now even more stressful for his wife and children than if he had stayed completely out of sight. Having a father in the house does not guarantee an intact family.

Today children wait for mothers as well as fathers to come home from long days at work. But fathers more than mothers are often peripheral in their families even when they are home, spending much of their time in the study or the garage, or with sports or a hobby, or focusing exclusively on work, computer games, or television. Our families are not necessarily intact just because we live together in the same house.

The challenge for families—and for Marge and Phil—is to maintain connections, psychologically as well as physically. This used to happen at least at the evening dinner table for many families, but that ritual is now often replaced with grazing or eating alone, even when everyone is home. This is disturbing. Unless there is some time for being together psychologically—emotionally and cognitively—the psychological family may disappear. Without time for talking, laughing, arguing, sharing stories, and showing affection, we are just a collection of people who share the same refrigerator.

Psychological absence is also a phenomenon of immigrant families, and it especially affects young children. Often their

58   émigré parents and grandparents are homesick and melancholy, preoccupied with loved ones far away. In such cases they are emotionally unavailable to the children.

In immigrant families, then, both kinds of ambiguous loss—psychological and physical—can occur simultaneously in different generations. My own family experienced this double legacy through my maternal grandmother, Elsbeth, who in 1909 came willingly to the United States but was prevented from returning to Switzerland to visit her mother by harsh economic conditions during the Depression and by the impossibility of travel across the Atlantic during World War II. By all accounts, she never adjusted to life in America. Physically cut off from her mother, siblings, friends, and the Alps she so loved, Elsbeth never adapted to her new surroundings. "Her mind was always back in Switzerland," my mother would say. Freud probably would have labeled her chronic homesickness as "melancholia." Whatever the label, my grandmother's preoccupation with her physical loss created a psychological loss for her daughter, Verena (who was to become my mother). When I asked my mother how she coped, she told me this story:

> I could never reach her. When I'd come home from school—I was in third or fourth grade—Mother would be standing by the window in the door, motionless, always looking east. In her dialect, she said she was looking toward the "Heimatland." Breakfast dishes were still on the table, the beds unmade, and nothing ready for supper. Even then I knew her behavior wasn't right. Other mothers didn't act that way.
>
> As I got older, I noticed often that my mother wasn't all there. You could tell when her mind was in Switzerland. At first when she was like that, I would try to get her back. But she would get

mad, really mad, and take it out on us kids, mostly me. Once when I was ten, she threatened to kill herself, so I never bothered her again when she was like that. Eventually, she would go and lie down. Usually she'd be sick, so I just went ahead and did the housework and took care of my brothers.

The causes of Elsbeth's depression and melancholia were no doubt multiple, but being physically cut off from her mother and sisters when she most needed their support clearly added to her suffering. She became dysfunctional and was psychologically unavailable to her own daughter. The young Verena had to fend for herself.

When I finished eighth grade, I went to work for another woman as a "hired girl."[7] She taught me to cook and keep a clean house. She was not really motherly, but at least she talked to me and taught me things. I saw that family life could be different. When I was eighteen, I married a Swiss immigrant from the neighboring farm. He was good to me. I had a better life after I married and it wiped out the other. I look at it this way. It wasn't my mother's fault. She never, never got used to living in this country. Tied to a husband and children and with no money of her own, she was stuck. She couldn't go back, and she couldn't move on.

Like Elsbeth and Verena, other émigré parents and their children must often find their own ways to cope with ambiguous loss. Such loss is not usually addressed by medical, religious, or legal experts, and friends and relatives are usually not aware that such a phenomenon exists. The devastation wrought by unresolved grief is only intensified when no one validates it. Neighbors say things like, "What are you complaining about? You are lucky to be here." "You have your husband and children; why do you need anyone else?" "You

60   should just be grateful that your mother is alive—even though you'll never see her again." And on and on. Partial losses are not readily understood by others, and thus are even more confusing for those experiencing them.

Physicians often prescribe anti-depressants for patients with symptoms of unresolved grief. But medication, though certainly beneficial in many cases, may not be enough to help family members who must live with ambiguous loss. If professional therapists are to help people resume a healthy, productive life, they must listen to their stories, ask about the stress they are experiencing, and not just focus on the obvious symptoms—or the symptom-bearer alone. Certainly routine assessments by trained clinicians are necessary when people exhibit physical or psychological symptoms, but assessments of their family life must also be taken into account. The family is our nearest environment; thus the losses, clear and ambiguous, that occur in a family are especially important in determining how best to help those struggling to move beyond their pain.

⚔ 4 ⚔

Mixed Emotions

> Even the normal person feels, as it were, two souls in his breast.
> Eugen Bleuler, *Textbook of Psychiatry*

PEOPLE EXPERIENCING AMBIGUOUS LOSS ARE FILLED WITH conflicting thoughts and feelings. They dread the death of a family member who has been hopelessly ill—or mysteriously missing for a long time—but they also hope for closure and an end to the waiting. They may even feel anger at someone they love for keeping them in limbo, only to be consumed with guilt for having such thoughts. The tension that results from conflicting emotions, especially when family members' unresolved grief is not acknowledged, becomes so overwhelming that they are frozen in their tracks. They cannot make decisions, cannot act, and cannot let go.

For more than a century, the concept of ambivalence has been central in psychology and psychiatry, focusing primarily on contrasting impulses in the psyche.[1] It is generally understood to indicate a conflict between positive and negative feelings toward a person or set of ideas. The resolution of ambivalence essentially hinges on helping a person to recog-

62 nize his or her conflicting feelings. From the psychological view, the problem is that some feelings about a relationship are usually more accessible to an individual's consciousness than are others.

But sociology provides another perspective.[2] According to this view, ambivalence results from mixing the elements of cognition (such as social definitions of roles and status) and emotion (which includes conditioning and learned behavior). Thus from this perspective, ambivalence can result from the ambiguity of not knowing who is included in the structure that is supposed to be one's family. Conflicting impulses that may exist inside the psyche are often a consequence of this uncertainty.

Ambivalence is often intensified by deficiencies outside the family—officials cannot find a missing person or medical experts cannot clearly diagnose or cure a devastating illness. Because of the ambiguity, loved ones can't make sense out of their situation and emotionally are pulled in opposing directions—love and hate for the same person; acceptance and rejection of their caregiving role; affirmation and denial of their loss. Often people feel they must withhold their emotions and control their aggressive feelings because social norms dictate that becoming upset is inappropriate and will only bring further harm to the missing person, demented elder, or comatose child. This is the bind, especially for women, who are most often caught in caregiving or waiting roles.

Mixed emotions are compounded when a separation involves the potential of irretrievable loss. When there is a chance that we will never see a loved one again, we protect ourselves from the prospect of losing that person by becoming ambivalent—holding our spouse at arm's length, picking a fight with a parent, or shutting a sibling out even while he or she is still physically present. Anticipating a loss, we both cling to our loved ones and push them away. We resist their leaving and at the same time want to be finished with the goodbye.

Many wives of military pilots who flew dangerous missions over Vietnam told me that the last few days of their rest and recuperation reunions in Hawaii or Bangkok often ended badly. The couple would fight or one would withdraw, going off alone or simply staring into space. "It was as if we separated even before he left," one woman said. And then her guilt set in.

I see a similar dynamic with people who are about to say goodbye to loved ones in less extreme situations—for example, when a child goes off to college. This, too, is ambiguous loss. Every fall many parents experience ambivalence about this transition; they are simultaneously happy and sad to see their children leave home. As if to make the parting easier, parents sometimes instigate fights with their children just before they leave. Impending losses result in ambivalent thoughts and feelings even in everyday situations.

Although conflicted feelings such as these are normal in human relationships, they can be overwhelming when the whereabouts of a loved one remain ambiguous for years. Consider the example of a mother who gave up her baby. In the 1940s, deeply in love with a sailor who got killed before they could marry, the woman gave birth to a baby boy, whom she gave up for adoption. A half century later, she concedes in a television interview that she "thought about this child every day for the next fifty years." "Do you then

64 regret your decision to give up your baby?" the interviewer asks. "Oh . . . I have mixed feelings about that," she responds. She explains that her mixed feelings come from her fear of what society would have done to her son. In the 1940s the town would have shunned a child with an unmarried mother. Her son would have been stigmatized. "So, I'm glad he had a chance to grow up in a regular family," she says, but in the same breath adds, "I never stopped thinking about him!"

This woman's constant ruminations about her child were an indicator of ambivalence, but this time, the ambivalence was fueled by social norms, not psychological deficiency. Through persistent inquiry years later on the Internet, she finally found her son—who, coincidentally, had also been searching for her. After their reunion, she said, "When you give up your baby for adoption, it's like the first few chapters of your life are missing. Now I have the lost pages to my life story. I feel complete."[3]

Ambiguous loss blurs the tidy boundaries of a couple or a family, causing people to question their most intimate relationships. Who is in and who is out remains cloudy. Fear and anger mix with confusion. As a family therapist, I often hear questions such as, "Am I still a mother?" "Do I have a husband or not?" "Am I really married?" Even within families not experiencing ambiguous loss there is often no strong consensus of who constitutes family. Just ask each of your children or your mate to draw a circle representing the family boundary. Then ask them to draw inside that circle everyone they see as inside the family, indicating how close together they see each member of the family. You may be surprised by the variation. Determining who is in and who is out of one's family is, in the end, an individual matter, but if a couple or a family is to function without conflict, they must come to some agreement as to who makes up their inner circle. Perceptions will vary greatly from family to family (for example, in remarried families versus first-married families) and from culture to culture, but as long as there is some understanding among family members, people can often avoid the devastating effects of ambiguous loss.

Many voices within a family make such determinations, but clearly some have more influence than others. Whereas a child may see both parents as inside the family, the parents—especially if they are at war with each other—may disagree vehemently and see each other as out of the family. This can occur regardless of their status as married, divorced, remarried, or never married. Often in such cases one parent will not, for example, attend the child's birthday party if the other parent is present. On holidays such children, even as adults, must frantically make the rounds to multiple homes because their parents cannot tolerate being in each other's presence even for a few hours. In the end, the child becomes ambivalent about seeing either parent because the tension is so high. Caught between warring parents, the child is unable to move. Family boundaries do not always have to be agreed upon, but if such extreme differences in perceptions persist, the ambiguity eventually creates ambivalence and, subsequently, troubled relationships.

Just ask the members of remarried families that include "his children," "her children," and "their children," and are made even more complex by the addition of kin, in-laws, and multiple grandparents. Not surprisingly in such situations, family members often perceive family boundaries differently.

66   In remarried families, a child whose parent has a new spouse may view the absence of the noncustodial parent as a loss, albeit a confusing one. Divorce settlements that split brothers and sisters may also constitute such losses for children. The uncertainty of who is still there for them can lead to ambivalence. Is this my brother or just my father's girlfriend's son? Is this my mother or just my father's wife? Is my mother's new husband now my father or only her husband? Nothing is clear, so emotions remain mixed.

Ambivalence can damage the fabric of the family even when there is no divorce. Sometimes there are dangerous consequences. The family of a fifteen-year-old girl who had twice set her mother's bed on fire was referred to me. Trish was institutionalized for treatment and was about to be released. I was to prepare the family for her return home. Everyone except her father was nervous about having her in the house again. Mother and father had a relationship full of conflict and criticism. They were from different cultures—he from Greece and she from the midwestern United States. They differed greatly in their expectations of what marital and family relationships should be like. He believed in patriarchy and felt he was in charge even though he was gone much of the time. She was able to manage the household and children when he was gone, but she hungered for more of his company. "Mother doesn't have much fun," one of the children said. Mother agreed. Dad said that when he wasn't working or going to professional conferences, he liked to spend his time visiting his brothers, who were also in this country. His wife sighed, "I'm all for the family—but *which* family? While he is with them, I am stranded at home. I can't get away from the kids very often." I asked, "What would you like to do if the kids could take care of themselves for a short time?" Her response was immediate, "I'd really like my husband to say, 'Let's go away for a weekend!'" Her husband acted as if he didn't hear her, and responded with a non sequitur, "I want my family to always be with me when I am home—all together. I feel good when we are all together." I asked him if he wished that this family was more like the family he lost when he came to the United States. For the first time, his eyes grew damp. But he quickly collected himself. "There, my father was the law."

The fire-setting daughter was not the only worrisome aspect of this family. There were other signs of serious trouble: the eldest son was striking his mother when she didn't do what he wanted. The father didn't back his wife up by disciplining the son, nor did he tell him to cease such behavior. Mother felt that no one was in her corner and she was scared, especially now that her daughter was about to return. Father wanted his daughter home, and he saw himself as the final authority.

Because this was a difficult case, I enlisted the help of a cotherapist. I also asked Carl Whitaker at the University of Wisconsin for a consult. "The Electra Complex," he muttered.[4] "But be sure to look at the whole picture." Whitaker believed that the systemic context was key in treating individual problems.

When the family arrived for their next session, my cotherapist and I were surprised to see that Trish was there with her family. She had been sent home for a trial visit in spite of her mother's fears. With all this immediate danger, I wondered how I could justify spending the session exploring unconscious desires and sexual symbols with this young Electra.

68   But as we talked, Trish revealed a crucial piece of information. She casually mentioned something about "her first fire."
I assumed she meant the first time she set her mother's bed on
fire. "No," she said, "I mean the first fire! The one at summer
camp, when my clothes caught on fire. I was roasting marsh-
mallows around the campfire. I got burned all over."

I took a deep breath. No one had mentioned that fire
before. It was not in any of the reports I had received from the
institution. I called and asked if her therapists knew about
this fire. "No," they said. This externally caused trauma that
threw the family into turmoil was almost missed because the
focus was on Trish's psyche and not on her experience or that
of the family as a whole.

We spent weeks talking about this traumatic event, but
more than the fire, the family's pain appeared to center on
ambiguous losses. Mother brought up the old anger she felt
toward her husband for being away at a convention during
the horrific first days when Trish was in the hospital with
third-degree burns. She needed him there. On the day when
the burned skin had to be taken off—an excruciatingly painful experience for Trish—he called and said he could not get
home, so Mom had to face their daughter's ordeal alone. She
never forgave her husband for not being there for her and her
daughter at such a difficult time.

There were several approaches a therapist could have used
with this family, but one thing was clear: the first fire was not
the fault of any family member. Yet the pain in this family was
from more than the trauma of the daughter's third-degree
burns. Everywhere, there was uncertainty and the pain of
abandonment—the parents were not really there for each
other or for their children. Although the problems in this

family were complex, ambiguous loss was clearly causing a good deal of their pain. The father was not physically there for his wife and children; when he did come home, he was authoritarian and thus still remote. Adding to his psychological absence was his deep preoccupation with his family of origin, and the ambivalence he sometimes felt about being with his own wife and children. He missed his homeland and his family, yet he raised issues of unresolved anger with his authoritarian father, now out of reach. His wife's ambiguous losses centered on being married to a husband who was mostly absent—often physically, and almost always psychologically. The children's ambiguous losses stemmed from having a father who was psychologically absent even when he was home, as well as a mother who was constantly preoccupied with her husband's unavailability. Finally, the entire family was detached, unable to speak and interact freely without threat of abuse or abandonment. No one was really there for anyone else. The parents as well as the children were ambivalent about closeness and distance, love and hate, expressing anger or hiding it—until it exploded in dangerous ways.

More commonly, children and parents show their mixed feelings about absence and presence in less dangerous ways. It is normal to have mixed feelings about one another—parents wanting to keep their children close and at the same time wanting them to fly free; children wanting to leave, but also wanting to stay. But in most cases, the ambivalence is conscious. We talk about it; we even make jokes about it. Communication saves us from the mixed emotions that often result from ambiguity.

Sometimes, however, we may not want a clear answer about the absence or presence of a person we love. When this

70   happens, the ambiguity thrives. Take the story of *M. Butterfly,* in which Gallimard, a French diplomat in China, maintains a twenty-five-year love affair with an opera singer he assumes is a woman.[5] Verification of gender would have been possible, and in fact at one point Butterfly offers to quiet Gallimard's curiosity by undressing in front of him. But Gallimard refuses, not really wanting to know the facts. His ambivalence about his own sexual orientation creates a comfortable vagueness about Butterfly's gender and maintains the ambiguity inherent in their relationship. For a man who cannot accept the idea that he might love another man, not knowing is safer than knowing.

In the play, which is based on a true story, facts were available but unconsciously not wanted. Each time Gallimard had a suspicion, Butterfly would lower her eyes as if to say, "I am shy, as is the Chinese custom for a woman, but if you insist, I will lie down naked in full view of you . . . because I love you so much." This was the ultimate double bind, and Gallimard always backed off. Butterfly even presented Gallimard with a child he believed was his own. Whether their relationship was maintained for so long because of latent homosexuality on the part of Gallimard or darn good acting on the part of Butterfly, the facts were never apparently taken in by Gallimard while the two were living together for more than two decades.

Although I have not seen couples with ambivalence as extreme as Gallimard's—or Betty Cox's in her relationship with the jazz musician Billy Tipton (born Dorothy Lucille Tipton)—I do see couples and families who experience mixed emotions because the absence or presence of a family member is veiled. Such families are uncertain about the status of a loved one in the family, but others are not. People will say, "Open your eyes! Your father shouldn't drive anymore; he doesn't even know where he is going." "Your mother is not just getting old and forgetful; she has dementia. She should not be allowed to use the stove anymore." "Your father is missing and will never be found. Give up the search." Such news is not easy to hear, for it means that the loss is irretrievable. Understandably, we prefer ambivalence to a resolution of grief because at least for the moment, it preserves the status quo and leaves us free of guilt. No one can be blamed because nothing is yet lost.[6]

There are also contemporary twists in the interaction between ambivalence and ambiguity. As medical technology makes advances both in diagnosing diseases and in identifying those who will get a particular illness, people must decide how much they want to know. For example, medical tests are now available for such serious illnesses as breast cancer, prostate cancer, HIV/AIDS, Lou Gehrig's disease, Huntington's disease, and Alzheimer's. Although testing can clearly identify those who have a disease or are likely to get it, many people refuse the tests because they are ambivalent about knowing the results. They prefer ambiguity to knowing their future. Not knowing allows them the possibility of hope that they may avoid the dreaded disease. But choosing to stay in the dark comes at a price. Consider the son of a Huntington's patient who refuses to be tested even though he has a fifty-fifty chance of not getting his father's disease. Despite the odds, he refuses to marry or have children. His ambivalence about knowing his fate prevents him from developing a close relationship and making a personal commitment. Eventually, his girlfriend gives up and leaves him. Although he has

72   shielded himself from potential anguish, he has forfeited a chance at happiness.

In most cases of ambiguous loss, however, people actively seek information that will clarify their situation, but there is no information available. I have seen families of missing soldiers, mates of patients with AIDS or Alzheimer's, and parents of missing children desperately seek information about the status of their loved ones. They are not resisting reality; the facts are simply not available. In such situations the ambiguity feeds ambivalence. People don't know whether to act married or single, to hope or to give up, to hate or to love the missing person, to leave or to stay, to give up or to wait. Family members of patients with Alzheimer's are often both angry and sad: angry at the demands of caregiving, and sad because they are losing a loved one. To be unable to make a single connection with someone with whom we have had a lifetime of meaningful conversations would give rise to ambivalence in the best of us. But such mixed feelings can freeze people in place if they block the ability to make decisions for change.

This was the case with a couple who spent their winters in Florida. When asked to describe the most stressful events that had occurred in the past year in relation to her husband's Alzheimer's, Mrs. Beal described their trip back from Florida in the spring. Mr. Beal, who was driving, had become confused and lost as they traveled through Chicago. Although clearly frightened by this experience, Mrs. Beal admitted that her husband would be driving again on their next trip to Florida. When I asked why, her mixed feelings became apparent. She said she didn't know how to tell her husband that he shouldn't drive anymore, but then noted that she herself had never driven the car on long trips and was not sure she could. Rather than getting some driving lessons to update her skills, Mrs. Beal remained ambivalent and supported a dangerous status quo.

Although living with the combination of ambiguity and ambivalence can lead to problems, it doesn't have to. Once the family talked about the situation and what Mrs. Beal's taking over the wheel would mean, they all understood that she had to drive, for the sake of safety. Her daughter offered to give her a refresher course in freeway driving, and they practiced on Sundays when traffic was light. The sixty-four-year-old Mrs. Beal found she could do the driving and do it well. She enlisted the help of an auto club to map out her route, and she and her husband returned to Florida once again, but this time, she was the driver. Thanks to her children's support, she was no longer ambivalent about her new role.

Hearing this story, I was reminded of how people from less patriarchal cultures solve such problems. The Ojibway and the Canadian Cree tell many stories about children with absent parents. In these stories, the absence of a parent is not as devastating as it might be because in most situations grandparents will adopt the children when the parents are gone. Also, aunts and uncles fill in as parent figures when needed. Perhaps if we could be more flexible about family roles and who the family is, we would have less ambivalence toward loved ones who are partially absent or present.

Perhaps one of the most instructive examples of flexible family boundaries—one accessible to children as well as to adults—can be found in Steven Spielberg's film *ET: The*

74   *Extra-Terrestrial.*[7] In this film a lonely ten-year-old boy named Eliot meets a gentle alien. A deep friendship develops, making up for Eliot's absent father and an overly busy mother. ET and Eliot connect, but ET pines for home. When Eliot realizes ET will die if he can't return to his people, he is ambivalent. He wants him to live, but he doesn't want him to go. "We could grow up together; I wouldn't let anyone hurt you," he says to ET. But ET's breathing is labored; he is near death; he stops breathing. But he revives! Eliot overcomes his ambivalence and swings into action, rushing ET to where a spaceship will come for him. "Home," ET says. Eliot knows this means goodbye, but he also knows that this is the only way ET can stay alive. When it's time to go, ET says sadly to Eliot, "Come." Eliot says, "Stay," meaning that he cannot leave. They both sigh. There is a long embrace with warm purring sounds coming from ET. They look at each other; Eliot says, "Stay with me." And then a profound thing happens. ET touches his lighted finger to Eliot's forehead and says, "I'll be right here." They separate, and ET slowly walks into the spaceship. The door closes. He is physically gone. But Eliot is both happy and sad. He has lost ET's physical presence, but he has discovered that the experience of connection has transformed him, for ET will forever be present in his thoughts.

Today the film *ET* is used by pediatric psychiatry researchers as an emotionally evocative stimulus to study changes in the heart rate, respiration rate, and emotional reactivity of asthmatic children.[8] Researchers hope to determine the relationship between stressful family dynamics, parental discord, and children's emotional and physiologic functioning. It is interesting to note that Spielberg said the story of *ET* was in his head for decades, perhaps unconsciously—a childhood fantasy of a special friend who rescues a young boy from the sadness of his parents' divorce. Indeed, the film *ET* is a metaphorical example of the emotional pain caused by experiences of ambiguous loss mixed with ambivalence.

There may indeed be a link between ambiguous loss, ambivalence, and an asthmatic child's response to the goodbye that takes place in *ET*. Like Eliot, asthmatic children report feeling both happy and sad when ET is leaving, and their physiology reflects a destabilization in autonomic nervous system functioning—an emotional upheaval. In addition, children's oxygen saturation, an indirect reflection of their pulmonary function, is also unstable during the goodbye scene. Researchers attribute these findings to mixed and conflicted emotions. With substantiation from research, the linking of ambiguous loss and ambivalence to physiological reactions could lend insight into prevention and therapy for children who have physical illnesses that are influenced by emotional stress.

Focusing only on people's psyches and egos does not always make their ambivalence go away; it might even make them feel as if their symptoms are their own fault. While the traditional approach to the resolution of ambivalence hinges on helping people recognize the two sides of their feelings, the external situation must also be addressed when mixed feelings emerge out of an ambiguous loss. Ideally, the ambiguity would clear up: the missing child would be found, a mate lingering with an excruciatingly painful terminal illness would mercifully die, the bones of a missing soldier would

76   finally be located and honored. Such clarity, however, is not
always possible. Failing that, the ambiguous loss needs to be
validated and labeled as being responsible for the ambivalent
feelings. Knowing that under such circumstances mixed feelings are normal, and knowing the situation is not their fault,
people are less resistant to therapy or interventions aimed at
helping them recognize the full range of their feelings.

⤙ 5 ⤚

Ups and Downs

JOHN'S WIFE, SARAH, WAS IN THE ADVANCED STAGES OF Alzheimer's disease when my research assistant and I went to interview John at his home in a small midwestern town. She was lying in a hospital bed in the living room, curled up in a fetal position. A Hoyer lift was next to her bed to ease the task of lifting and turning her. Because Sarah could no longer swallow food without choking, John had just made the difficult decision to feed her through a tube.

I had come to this couple with a theory in hand—in this case, the rollercoaster model of family stress. Surely this man had just had the crisis of his life, having to decide whether to let his demented wife die of starvation or allow a tube to be inserted into her stomach for feeding, thereby extending her life indefinitely. I asked John if this was the lowest point for him in his family's struggle with Alzheimer's. I assumed his response would be "Yes." It was not. Instead, his answer challenged what I and others have written about family stress and crisis.[1]

John said that the loss of his wife was progressing in steps, and her inability to swallow food was just one in a series of many crises during her illness. "What were the others?" I asked. "Here, let me show you," he said, taking my pencil. John drew what looked like a downward staircase; then he labeled each stair as a new crisis. At each step downward, he said, he had felt confused, and for a time he hadn't known what to do to control the situation.

At the top of the staircase drawing, John identified the first crisis: "She got lost in her own house," he said. He had panicked and not known what to do. After a while, he had gathered his courage and taken Sarah to the doctor. The diagnosis had been what he feared—probable Alzheimer's disease. "But now," he said, "we knew what we were facing. I took over the management of the household and we kept going."

The second crisis came when John realized that he and Sarah could no longer take trips. Traveling had been the highlight of their life together, and so this was a major loss. Feelings of sadness were mixed with feelings of being trapped. As time went on, however, John adapted to the idea that his wife would never travel again; he revised his idea of travel to include day trips for himself during which he went fishing or played golf.

Just about the time he recovered from the no-travel crisis, there came another. On the third step in his drawing, John wrote: "Sarah wanders at night." Because of her nocturnal ramblings, he was no longer getting the sleep he needed; he was constantly searching for Sarah and trying to get her back to bed. This crisis, too, was finally managed, this time with medical help and medication for Sarah. But there were more crises to come, and fewer high points on his emotional ride. The fourth step John labeled "Incontinence" ("That really hit me"), the fifth, "Pneumonia" ("Sarah almost died"), the sixth, "She doesn't know me anymore," and the seventh, "Tube feeding." "This [last] is the hardest one," John explained, "because we know this is the last stage before death." Indeed, the crisis John was experiencing when I went to visit him was the last plummet in a long series of ups and downs. Finally, he pointed to the last step: "This will be death," he said. "We aren't there yet." Five years after I had this conversation with John, Sarah was still living.

Responses like John's are important because they show that even healthy caregivers find it difficult to remain in control of their own lives in the face of long-term ambiguous losses. Lack of mastery over one's life increases not only perceptions of helplessness but *real* helplessness. For many, this leads to depression. But from people like John, we can learn that coping with a disease like Alzheimer's need not be devastating. John faced each crisis, made decisions to bring it under control, took respite and recreation during the calmer periods, and continually accepted help from his neighbors and community.

Caregivers like John often find that they are able to manage the day-to-day stress of tending to a loved one whose status is ambiguous by connecting with something stable in their lives. For John, it was golf every Thursday and church on Sunday. For others, it could be another kind of social or spiritual support, or friends who help or listen. But meaningful connections can't happen if people in the community never validate an ambiguous loss as a traumatic loss. John was fortunate because his neighbors knew what he was experiencing. They realized from visiting his house that his wife was slipping away in stages. They knew he needed to maintain

80 friendships and activities outside the home, and that by doing so he was not being disloyal to his wife.

Unfortunately, not all communities are so understanding when it comes to a caregiver's needs. More often, the tendency is to criticize or withdraw from those who need help. Other people's losses remind us of our own vulnerability, and thus can be anxiety-provoking. What if we found ourselves in John's position? Or in his wife's? Could we handle the pressure? Alternatively, neighbors and friends might withdraw because the level of help needed is simply too high to sustain when the ambiguous loss goes on for a long time.

It is important to realize that the stressful fluctuations John experienced will to varying degrees affect most of us at one time or another. Nonetheless, it is possible to find relief and eventually manage the situation, despite the likelihood of another downward dip—another temporary period of helplessness. The human experience is never one of certainty or predictability, but with the support of caring family members, friends, and neighbors, as well as the comfort that some derive from spiritual beliefs, we learn to hang on during such inevitable emotional rides.

In this painful process, one of the complications is denial. Sometimes loved ones faced with the threat of loss refuse to see what others see, to hear what others hear, and to acknowledge a painful reality. Denial is most often considered a defense mechanism, and so it is easy to see why people dealing with uncertainty would want to protect themselves from thinking the worst. Not knowing for sure if, for example, a loved one classified as missing in action is really dead, or if a family member diagnosed as terminally ill will really die, people understandably remain hopeful. Hopefulness is, after all, a characteristic of optimism, and it can serve a useful purpose when there is ambiguous loss. This was the case with the Klein family. The following ad in the November 12, 1989, issue of the *Minneapolis Star Tribune* caught the eye of a colleague who brought it to my attention:

> KEN, DAVID & DAN KLEIN. MISSING since Nov. 10, 1951. We are still waiting to hear from you . . . Mom and Dad. [The notice ends with two telephone numbers.]

We made an appointment and drove to Monticello, Minnesota, to interview this couple, and they told us their story.[2]

In 1951, three of their four boys, ranging in age from four to six, disappeared from a playground near their house where they routinely went to play. (The fourth had stopped to fix a broken shoelace, and when he reached the park, his brothers were gone.) Two of the boys' wool caps were later found in the Mississippi River. In the agonizing weeks after their boys disappeared, Betty and Kenny Klein kept hoping it was all a nightmare that would soon be over. Betty elaborated, "Every time a car went by slow, or we heard a door slam in the night . . . we thought it was our boys coming home . . . It was very hard . . . you don't know how many tears were shed, you know . . . I used to sit out there on that back step and cry like my heart was breaking . . . And I often said, uh, if you ever had a broken heart, I had it."

More than forty years later, the Kleins still advertise for the missing boys to come home. Some therapists might call this "illusion construction" and encourage such self-protective behavior, because overly optimistic judgments of the chances of success—the chances, for example, of finding missing loved

82   ones—tend to enhance, not harm, a family's adaptation to their loss.[3] But in reality, the Kleins' hopes may not be an illusion, for as recently as October 10, 1996, Doug Grow of the *Minneapolis Star Tribune* reported that a truckdriver from Arizona called and said he was David, one of the Kleins' missing sons. The man told the Kleins things that they thought only a family member would know; he said he would visit them the following summer. Their hopes were raised. But the man never came. Another son told the reporter, "The hopes of all of us soared for a while, but we don't get too carried away anymore."

For most of us, the tendency is to keep a relationship going, not to give it up. Once attached, we resist letting go, so that when someone we love mysteriously disappears, denial becomes an understandable response. In the case of the Kleins, as with many families of missing loved ones, the reality of occasional reports and sightings keeps hope alive. What I see in the Kleins is an expression of hopeful optimism rather than unconscious denial.

Even families whose loss is more gradual cling to hope as a defense against pain. I remember reading the autobiography of a woman with terminal cancer whose daughter denied the gravity of her mother's illness. The writer, in the advanced stages of cancer, describes a conversation with her daughter, who heretofore had resisted the fact that her mother was dying. Their words illustrate the difficulty of giving up hope:

> "Are you more ready now for me to die?" I ask my daughter. "More ready than before?" She is very still. During my illness she has grown from sixteen to twenty . . . *"Ready,"* she says, finally, "is an inhuman word. Let's say I'm more familiar with the idea." We cry.[4]

The daughter had moved from denial to a reluctant acceptance, a healthy process of grieving that can begin only when the ambiguity lessens. In this case, the mother helped clarify her status; she herself labeled what was imminent—her death. With such clarity, denial is eroded and hope can shift to a more realistic goal. The daughter no longer hopes for her mother's recovery, but for a death without pain.

But sometimes there isn't enough time to let go. My sister Ellie always wore beautiful bright colors, heavy perfume, and big jewelry. She was two years older than I, and if other children picked on me when I first went to school, they had to deal with her. For eighteen years, until she graduated from high school and went off to teachers' college, we shared a bedroom in the family's cramped farmhouse. Back then, late at night when she was asleep, I'd listen to radio broadcasts from Chicago, imagining my escape to the big city. But Ellie never cared about cities and lived her whole life near our hometown in Wisconsin. She became a master teacher in the local high school, highly respected by the several generations she taught. Her only escape from the confines of smalltown life was the yearly summer tour she led to Europe. She had ingeniously found her own way out.

My own exit was not so graceful. I exploded out with a divorce and left for good. But no matter where we were, Ellie and I talked on the phone weekly as well as on the rare holidays when we weren't together. We watched out for each other during times of pregnancy, childbirth, and childrearing, when her babies and mine were often mixed into one big family. We cared for each other's broods so we could each have time for our own pursuits—mostly finishing college degrees. It never occurred to me that we would not grow old together.

84   The last phone call I made to my sister was from Rome, where I was attending a family therapy conference. My daughter had called to tell me Ellie was sick, but not to worry. I called anyhow. "I hear you're in the hospital with pneumonia," I said. "How are you doing?" Silence. "I have lung cancer," she said quietly. I froze. My breath stopped. "Oh, no!" I pleaded. "That can't be. You don't smoke. You haven't even been sick. It was just a month ago that we were hiking in the Rockies together, and you outwalked me!" Silence. Then with resolve, she said, "I'm going to try to lick this thing." I grabbed at that hope. "I'll come right home. I'll see you Sunday."

Five weeks later, we buried my sister—in a bright red dress and wonderful jewelry.

During the less than six weeks that Ellie was so sick, the family was on an agonizing ride of ups and downs. One day she was better, the next she couldn't breathe, then the doctors said the chemotherapy was taking effect, then they said the cancer had spread to the lining of her heart, then some good news from the lab about the oxygen levels in her blood being higher, and then, while sitting up in a chair one autumn afternoon watching *Oprah,* she died. Crash. Still denying the seriousness of her cancer, we never really said goodbye.

While denial can sometimes be healthy when it helps families to maintain their optimism, it is harmful when it invalidates or renders people powerless. In such cases, denial takes two dramatically opposing forms, both of which are troublesome. At one extreme, people deny that anything is lost or threatened and act as if nothing has changed. A bride-to-be whose mother has end-stage renal disease insists that her mother, who does not "look" sick, can sew six bridesmaid's dresses as well as her bridal gown. The son of a seventy-year-old man with Alzheimer's disease says his father is just forgetful and that there is no reason for him to stop driving a car. A woman whose husband left her five years ago says it is just a matter of time until he comes to his senses and returns. For various reasons, people who deny that anything is wrong are not ready to hear the truth. They defend themselves by unconsciously opting for the status quo: things are as they always were; nothing is going to change.

At the other extreme, people act as if their loved one is totally gone from their lives. A person with AIDS or cancer is ignored as if already dead, is no longer visited or touched. A family throws a schizophrenic or alcoholic son out of the house and expects him to fend for himself. A man whose father has Alzheimer's disease says, "I get along with Dad fine as long as I think of him as a piece of furniture and just don't bump into him." A woman whose mate left her tells the children their father is dead. Such people clearly find comfort in absolute thinking, cutting themselves off completely from a loved one who is still living in order to avoid feeling the loss. But their inability to accept their new relationship with the sick or absent family member prevents them from making the most of the time they do have with their loved one, or from sustaining partial connections (as in divorce) that could benefit their children and grandchildren.

In the short term, however, absolute reactions may not always be dysfunctional. Just as being in shock temporarily protects the physical body after trauma, denial provides a temporary respite from the harsh psychological reality of a potential loss. It is also a way to reduce the distress that inevitably results from uncertain absence or presence. But

86   denial is a problem when, in its extremes, it prevents a transformation that would allow all those family members still present to move forward with their lives. It is also a problem when it invalidates the presence of a person who is still there. Finally, denial is a problem when it blocks creative options and choices for adapting to unclear losses. Frequently, such adaptations center on family rituals.

The Smith family came into therapy complaining angrily that the father, who suffered from Parkinson's disease, could no longer cook his traditional gourmet dinners on Sunday nights without making a mess in the kitchen and with the food. Together the family members, including the patient, were able to create a new and less demanding version of Dad's Sunday night treat—now popcorn and apples. But first they all had to break through their denial. They had to accept the fact that Parkinson's disease was now also a part of the family. Dad was not what he used to be, but he was still there. Once they accepted this fact, they could revise the ritual of a special Sunday night supper that had come to mean so much to them. There was hope; not everything had been lost.

This family and people like Betty and Kenny Klein are perhaps our best teachers for how to live with ambiguity with resilience rather than with the extremes of denial. They no longer deny their loss, nor do they stop working for—and hoping for—a positive outcome. They simultaneously hold two opposing ideas in their minds. For the Kleins, this involves thinking that the boys might still be alive somewhere—*and* acknowledging that they are probably dead. After their disappearance, Mrs. Klein said she would focus on the one child she had left at home, as well as on those who were to come. She describes this approach to ambiguity,

which academics would call dialectical thinking and others **87**
might call midwestern pragmatism:

> I guess this is probably what helped us, too, was the, we, we
> always knew we were needed for [our remaining son] . . . And
> I was pregnant with the baby, and the baby needed us. And so,
> you know, you can't put your hurts up front. You have to put
> them in the back and live on. And it doesn't mean you're gonna
> forget [the missing boys] . . . it just means you're, uh, you're
> taking care of today.[5]

It is now forty-seven years since the three little boys disappeared, but the vigil continues. Even though the odds are
small, a flicker of hope remains that at least one son might still
be alive somewhere. The Kleins' hope, however, is tempered
with reality. Betty explains:

> I don't know if I would be ready for them [the missing boys]
> [laughs]. You know what I mean. If you walked in a room and
> they said, "Well, this is your son," I wouldn't be ready for it . . .
> Because in my mind I guess I think it could happen, but it's a
> very slim chance, it happening, you know, so it would have to
> be this little slim chance, and [laughs] I would probably say, uh,
> "Well, I have to have a little proof," you know . . . The one that
> I think is . . . the safest way to get the proof is have a blood test
> . . . I think that'd be the best way to do it. Because that's pretty,
> pretty foolproof, although it isn't *completely* . . . but it's pretty
> close to it.[6]

While the Kleins found a way to balance hanging on with
letting go, many who experience unverified losses are unable
to adjust to their new situation. Gradual losses are often the
hardest to acknowledge. When a family member's health
fades bit by bit, for example, it is easy to miss the gradual
increments of loss. Day to day, the early evidence is very

88 subtle—a husband suffering from Alzheimer's will drop things more often, bump into things, forget what he said or repeat himself. Or in cases of estrangement, couples will gradually separate, with one spouse coming home later each night and then not at all. In either case, husbands and wives may stop talking to each other, stop celebrating holidays and birthdays together, stop touching and being intimate, develop separate lives, and finally cease interacting altogether. The relationship is dead.

Absolute thinking carries a high price. At either end of the spectrum—closing someone out too soon or acting as if nothing has changed—denial ultimately causes more rather than less distress for couples and families facing an ambiguous loss. It invalidates and separates them. Each person is alone in his or her private interpretation of who is absent and who is present. I've seen cases where people are so reluctant to accept a change in their family status that they are unable to function day to day. A rebellious teenager told me this story: "Dad and Mom got divorced years ago, but it's like Mom still expects Dad to come back. She doesn't have any friends of her own and worse yet, she won't make any decisions without trying to call him up to see what he thinks she should do . . . and then they just get into another big fight. She hangs up, cries—and then asks me what to do. What can I say? She just won't face the fact that Dad left."

Sometimes denial by one or more family members is disruptive of caregiving just when the patient—and other family members—most need their support. The Andersons illustrate this point.[7] Two generations gathered for an interview with my research assistant (I was behind the camera). Mr. and Mrs. Anderson lived in the family home; Beth drove over from her home about a mile away; Dave, newly divorced, had recently moved back into his parents' home and was attending graduate school. Two other adult children, Mary and Bill, lived in faraway cities and rarely came home anymore. They all had different perceptions of Dad's dementia and his absence or presence.

There was conflict throughout the interview. Mom and Beth both believed that Dad had dementia, and Dave believed the women were simply exaggerating signs of normal aging. In spite of a diagnosis of probable Alzheimer's, Dave denied that anything was wrong. He thought the others were over-reacting. "Dad has always been forgetful," he said. "I don't want you to treat him like a baby, you should keep his brain active. Everyone shouldn't think for him. You coddle him." Beth responded that it was Dave's moving back home that added to their mother's workload. "*You* are the one who is being coddled," she quipped.

The family continued to talk after the patient had been taken from the room. The conflict increased. Mom scolded Dave for his continued denial; she and her daughter were angry with him because he wasn't helping them care for Dad. Dave was angry with them for overprotecting his father. Tensions escalated as Beth tried to get her brother to see how their father had changed. She told Dave that the other day their Dad had put on one tennis shoe and one dress shoe. "He always was so meticulous about how he dressed," she said. Mrs. Anderson raised her voice impatiently, "You've got to face this, boy. This is a long-time thing and we are going to have to accept it." Dave resisted, "I don't want to accept this! If someone has a problem, you do. You don't just say he has this disease and give in. You go to the Mayo Clinic, you do

90   exercises, you improve his diet. You think you are helping him but you're just helping him to be weaker!"

The family's conflict continued at a high pitch, but then the mood suddenly shifted. Dave quietly conceded, "I know he has 'this disease.'" But he objected to giving in too soon; there might be a cure. Beth softened after her brother's concession and told Dave they needed him, "not to help Dad to be weak, but to help us with Dad." Dave became quiet and his voice cracked: "It's hard to see your parent, you know . . ." Beth interrupted. The interviewer stopped her. Dave was quiet for a bit and then said, "I know something is wrong."

After a silence, Beth said, "That's interesting. I never heard you say that before." "Well, obviously, something is wrong." Dave started to sob, covering his face. "I mean . . . what am I supposed to do, quit grad school so I can change his diapers?" Beth responded, "I don't think we are asking that." Dave continued, "I just want to find something to help him get over it, so we don't have to change everything . . . the way that life has been up to now. I just resent that . . . why can't we just keep going like we always were?" Beth became impatient, "Well, something *has* changed!" she snapped.

This family discussion illustrates the extremes of denial as well as the process of change that can take place when family members struggle together. Dave denied that anything was wrong; Mom and Beth acted as if Dad were already gone and didn't even let him speak for himself anymore. Still others, Mary and Bill, stayed away to avoid the pain. The family disagreed about Dad's status as absent or present, and so were unable to function as a unit during this difficult time.

"You've been trying to hold on and not change," the interviewer tells Dave. To Mrs. Anderson and Beth, he says,

"You've been trying to manage and work hard and let go." The empathy for differing views soothes the family and interrupts their bickering. It is a good time to end the interview. But just then, in the last moments, Dave turns to the interviewer and quietly asks, "Does it always . . . does it always get worse?"

Already, this family is beginning to come to a common understanding of what is lost through Alzheimer's disease, and to appreciate what the experience means to each family member individually. They are demonstrating a readiness to hear and to listen; perceptions are changing.[8]

When I deal with families suffering long-term ambiguous loss, my primary objective is to provide them with a place to sit and talk together. In traditional psychology, this is known as providing a safe holding environment. In addition, I give the family as much information as possible about the kind of loss they are experiencing in order to minimize denial and enable them to begin making some choices and decisions. For most couples or families, this kind of therapy—often called the psycho-educational approach—helps to unfreeze the coping process.

Admittedly, this approach assumes that family members have a high degree of cognitive and emotional functioning, but that is precisely my point. Most families, albeit not all, have more capacity to cope than professional therapists think they have. Thus it is essential that we ask each person involved about what is happening within the family. Is there any confusion about who is in and who is out of the couple or family relationships? Are there losses that have remained unclear? What does this mean to each of them? Once family members recognize and are given a name for the ambiguous

92   losses in their lives, and realize that their inability to move on is not their fault, they are less likely to use denial as a coping mechanism and more likely to be able to make important decisions. They regain some control over their lives and move forward once again.

In the end, denial is neither something to avoid nor something to advocate. It is a complex response that can be both functional and dysfunctional. What has become clear to me is that ordinary people—without benefit of analysis or therapy—can become more aware of their own responses and can often assess whether they are healthy or destructive. This is essential if they must live with unclear loss. Rather than labeling their denial as pathological, family therapists can help them to acquire information about their particular situation—be it a debilitating illness or another loss—as a way to cope with ups and downs, and then eventually all downs. It is the combination of optimism and realistic thinking that allows people to move ahead in spite of ambiguous loss, but first they need understanding and support from their own community—as well as from the professional community.

⋊ 6 ⋉

The Family Gamble

Herald, I didn't know if you was ever coming back . . . I stayed and waited there for five years before I woke up one morning and decided that you was dead. Even if you weren't, you was dead to me. I wasn't gonna carry you with me no more. So I killed you in my heart. I buried you. I mourned you. And then I picked up what was left and went on to make life without you.

August Wilson, *Joe Turner's Come and Gone*

FAMILY MEMBERS FACING A PAINFUL LOSS CANNOT DENY forever that something has changed. Eventually they are pressured, by a relative, a friend, or by circumstances themselves, to define the status of the missing person one way or the other. The family then makes their best guess, based on the available information, as to the probable outcome of their unclear loss. Is a son and brother missing in action in Vietnam likely to return home after twenty-five years? Is a father diagnosed with an inoperable tumor going to die? Will an adopted child benefit from a reunion with the biological mother or father? Will a missing father ever return? I call this the family gamble.

94   This judgment call is risky. Consider the family who gambles that the father is going to die. As a result of this conclusion, they close him out of their activities as though he is already dead. When the father goes into remission and lives, the family has to reorganize in order to take him back in again. Even with a positive outcome, this constant reordering of the family system is stressful—a family member is in, then out, then in again. If, by contrast, the family gambles that the father is going to live, making no preparations for loss or change, and then he dies, they also have to reorganize to let him go. Despite the uncertainty of their decision, however, a family is always better off making an educated guess about the status of their loss rather than continuing indefinitely in limbo. The family gamble is one way to get off the emotional rollercoaster of ambiguous loss.

Sometimes the family gamble pays off. Mrs. Lund visited her young comatose husband in a nursing home every day for five years. He had fallen from a horse and hit his head. "When you hear me, squeeze my hand," she'd say, even though doctors offered little hope that her husband would wake up. Each day she talked to him about their children and the details of country life. One day she was finally rewarded. He squeezed her hand. Gradually her husband returned to normal and has since come home.

But family gambles do not always end this way, nor do many people have the strength and determination to wait so patiently for so long. Such stories of miraculous recoveries in newspapers and magazines give hope to those who wait for things to return to the way they were rather than adapting to a changed reality. Mrs. Lund's long shot surprisingly paid off, but stories of ambiguous loss rarely end so well.

Sometimes families make the wrong decision, and others, out of fear of doing the same, refuse to take any risks at all. After years of searching for Mateo Sabog, a soldier declared missing in action, his family decided to give him up as dead. They asked the government to change his status from MIA to PKIA (presumed killed in action). His name on the Vietnam War Memorial was then preceded by a cross, indicating that he was dead. But after twenty-six years, Sabog turned up in a Social Security office in Georgia, where he was applying for benefits. It turns out that he finished his tour in Vietnam in 1970 but never arrived home in Georgia. Some people in California found him wandering and took him in. He stayed with them for twenty-six years. Regrettably, a cross still precedes his name at the Vietnam Memorial, but the official records are clear: they have been corrected to reflect that he was "found."[1] Though it is unlikely that other missing soldiers will return, families often cling to such stories while at the same time recognizing that the odds are against them.

In other cases, families are left wondering if they made the right decision, particularly when an illness or other period of waiting continues for a long time. A Texas father, with the help of his two adult daughters, decided to care for his wife at home.[2] She was in the last stages of Alzheimer's disease and, in addition to having difficulty swallowing food, she had pneumonia. He wasn't ready to let her go. But he also admitted, "I feel bad about my girls' giving up so much of their life. If it wasn't for the situation at home, my older daughter would be married right now." His younger daughter, who dropped out of college to come home and help and who has no boyfriend, was as concerned about her father as she was about her mother: "I worry about him coming out of this and

96   finding a reason to keep going." The gamble here is that two
       young adults who put things on hold to care for a dying
       parent may miss out on their own lives. Their father is hoping
       his daughters will be able to readjust and resume normal
       social lives once they no longer have to care for their mother,
       but his concern lingers.

       Gambling on absolute positions of either optimism or pes-
       simism is risky, but when the odds of a favorable outcome are
       high, family members should be encouraged to embrace
       hope, acting as if the loss is retrievable. In 1980, therapists
       used information gleaned from interviews with the families of
       prisoners of war and missing men to develop guidelines for
       working with the families of the Iranian hostages.[3] Since it
       was generally believed that the hostages would be safely
       returned from Iran, their families were advised to continue to
       act as if their missing loved ones were still present—to buy
       gifts for birthdays and holidays, to audio- or videotape all
       family celebrations, and to think of their family member as
       still in the family, so that when the hostages returned, their
       reintegration into family life would go smoothly. The families
       kept their boundaries symbolically open to minimize the loss
       for all concerned, and proceeded as if their loved ones would
       return. The gamble worked. On January 20, 1981, all of the
       Americans came home safely after spending 444 days as
       hostages in Tehran.[4]

       But when the probability of recovery is slim, as it is with
       Alzheimer's, terminal cancer, Huntington's disease, or a full-
       blown case of AIDS, it may be less reasonable to gamble on
       either extreme—on either treating the loss as complete or
       acting as if nothing has changed. A gradual process of letting
       go is the healthiest approach in such situations. Some aspects

of the missing person are lost forever, while others are very much present. The task for families is to remain aware of the difference. Neither the patients nor their loved ones are served by not living to the fullest their remaining days together, connecting where they still can before saying a final goodbye.

Children of patients with early-onset Alzheimer's and other heritable diseases live with the sobering possibility that they will get their parents' disease. The younger son of the airplane pilot who developed Alzheimer's at age forty says, "There's not much chance at all that I'm not going to get it. There's not a day or an hour in my life right now that I don't think about it. How am I going to start a family? Am I going to put my wife through what Mom is going through now? Should I have kids? Should I even get married?" His cousin, who is the young woman who quit college to take care of her mom, is more positive: "I just want to grab on to what comes along. But what if I really love someone? I can't imagine giving all that stuff up."[5]

And then there are those for whom the pain is so immobilizing that they are not even ready to take a risk. Another of the pilot's young sons was having a hard time. His mother explained, "He just can't handle it. It upsets him too much—even talking about insurance and a living will. Seeing his aunt that way and knowing in his heart that's what we have to look forward to [with his father for sure, and perhaps for himself, his brother, and his cousin] upsets him too much." As he watched his father, who could still eat and walk, the son said to his cousin, "I can't stick around. I can't see him on a day-to-day basis if he was [as sick as] your Mom. It would tear me up. My Dad and I were real close; it just tears

98   me up to watch it and I can't handle it anymore."[6] Note that the son mixes his tenses, using both past and present, a common indication of confusion about the status of a loved one who is still present but also partly gone.

The family gamble in such situations also affects the medical team caring for the patient. The family of a late-stage Alzheimer's patient who has pneumonia for the second time is angry when the doctors discourage heroic efforts. "That's the way doctors are. It is not worth their time if there is not a life to be saved—even though it's a life to us," says Wes's wife. Some families insist on treatment to keep their loved one alive despite knowing that the illness is terminal. They are simply not ready to say the final goodbye. Wes's wife expresses her frustration: "It makes me so mad that there's nothing we can do. The doctors don't seem to care. They feel like it's hopeless so they just give up."[7] She cuddles next to her demented husband, knowing that soon she will have to make life-and-death decisions. But for now, she gets comfort from being close to him, this man who is still her husband but not the man she married.

For families of people who are missing psychologically or physically, this process of gradually letting go is especially difficult because it has to take place exclusively in their minds. Just as Wes's wife knows that she, not the medical staff, will ultimately have to make the difficult decisions about her husband's life and death, the wives of missing soldiers who had no one to clarify their husbands' status as dead or alive had to do so for themselves. A wife was truly gambling when she finally asked for an official change in her husband's status from missing in action to presumed killed in action, for there is always the possibility that he could still be alive somewhere

and return home unexpectedly. Deciding to write the letter to
Washington requesting that her husband's status be changed
must have been very difficult—not unlike what family members of an Alzheimer's patient experience when they decide to
request that no resuscitation or heroic efforts be used anymore to keep their loved one alive.

The sociologist Erving Goffman has written that for events
like death, someone outside the family, such as a coroner, will
document the event to make it official. The family should not
be expected to perform that role.[8] But Goffman did not
consider the plight of families with ambiguous losses. They
are increasingly asked to do just that—to decide on the life
and death of a loved one. For many, this is a task beyond
human comprehension; for others, it is a risk they take in
order to move on with their own lives.

More subtle versions of the family gamble take place in the
ordinary transitions of family life. When children grow up
and leave home, their status as in or out of the family is often
confusing. Parents' best move in such situations is to define
their children's status as somewhere between absent and
present, as did one father whose son left home for college and
then returned:

> Since September, we've been in an odd sort of going-going-
> gone limbo. He's here, but he shouldn't be. He's here, but he
> won't be. And when he does go, he won't go far. Nobody at
> this address was prepared for that. We were prepared for lower
> food bills and higher phone bills, an empty chair at Thanksgiv-
> ing and an emotional welcome home at Christmas. We were
> prepared for what didn't happen. We're still trying to adjust to
> what did, still trying to figure out what the rules and expecta-

when they come back home—mothers may fear that they aren't fulfilling their duty if they don't take care of their offspring's every need. Social norms often reinforce that fear. Irene risked changing the mother-child relationship from one of nurturance to one of equality. Without negating her love for them, she insisted that her grown children care for themselves. Irene wagered that they would still love her, not for servitude, but for simply being there. The good news in this case was that Irene's gamble paid off. Her children did in fact move emotionally closer to her. And this had nothing to do with laundry. She and Fred found more time for each other, reviving activities they had enjoyed together in earlier years, such as fishing, dancing, and traveling.

The decision to change relationships is full of risks for the person who dares to take the first step. While the impetus begins with one person, however, the new patterns ultimately have to be practiced, not just in therapy, but at home and in real life with the people closest to us. Improvement is gradual; two steps forward and one backward is normal. The goal is to be at ease with solutions that are imperfect. The question of who is in, who is out, and how they are in or out of the family may never be completely clear, but if we can accept change, we can learn to live with the ambiguity.

The families that are most successful in dealing with change adopt a willingness to compromise. Rather than rigidly defending their favored solution to the problem of an uncertain loss, family members hear one another out and remain respectful of the opinions of their loved ones. They resolve to attack the problem and not one another. Like Irene and Fred, they refuse to continue tolerating what Alan Watts calls "the security of known misery." They are tired of the

status quo and seek change by reaching out and breaking
their isolation, interacting with others in their family and
community, talking, disagreeing, and compromising. Indeed,
according to George Herbert Mead, we need other people to
become our "looking glass" if we are to change perceptions
within the family.[10] Using the reactions of others—their
looks, their words, their emotions, and their touch—we co-
construct new realities. Even family members deeply en-
trenched in their loss and resistant to change will show a
greater willingness to accept a revised relationship with a sick
spouse or parent—or an absent child—once they have
reached out to others. Overcoming the solitude of ambiguous
loss is the first step on the road to healthy change.

Family life, like any organic life, depends on continuous
change. It's not a question of having the right answer—indeed, with ambiguous loss there may not be one. In the
absence of a perfect solution, we must risk creating the best
possible answer for the moment and know that the process of
revision will never stop as long as we live. Complicated losses
may seem hopeless and unresolvable, but the power to
change can never be taken from us.

In the end, therapists and physicians are not the ones who
can prescribe how people cope with partial losses. Cultures,
communities, neighborhoods, religious groups, and families
of origin do that. Because people who form families together
often come from different backgrounds, they may have different ideas about how or when to gamble. One indicator of
such differences in couples is their language. "Chance," for
example, is a word that doesn't exist in Hebrew; if you want
to talk about something in terms of chance, you have to resort
to the word "hazard."[11] In Italy and in Mexico, the word

104   "destiny" is used abundantly. The North American Indian women I talked with in northern Minnesota and Quebec spoke of "harmony with nature" and "spiritual acceptance." I never heard them use the term "catastrophic illness." They did not perceive as a failure the dementia of an elder who has lived a full life. Instead, they saw the deterioration of an elder as completing the circle of life, one that should be celebrated and accepted. They had no need for the family gamble.

Yet when cultures clash, as often happens in cases of immigration, the family's understanding of absence and presence and their definition of family become more challenging. Li's story is not uncommon in a country where there are many immigrants. She is an Asian-American woman who was pregnant with her first child. Her Seattle obstetrician recommended folic acid, multi-vitamins, and a diet rich in calcium. Her mother in Taiwan called her weekly to tell her which folk remedies to take and what to eat. Wanting a healthy baby, Li was torn between the old and the new. She decided to hedge her bets by honoring her mother's wishes as well as following the doctor's advice.

After the baby arrived, Li found she needed to revise some of the rituals and customs celebrated in her family so that they could be shared with her new baby and husband. She said this would make her feel as if some of her extended family were present. When she had left Taiwan to become an American, she had wanted to cut herself off from her extended family and their customs. But when she became a mother, she found that the loss of family ties was glaring. "The books, the nursery rhymes, the lullabies are all wrong here," she said. So she revised and merged, continuing the songs and stories her mother had passed on to her when she was a child, but adding

Mickey Mouse and other American icons to the repertoire. **105** As her child grew, she and her husband merged aspects of Christmas—a tree, a turkey, and toys—with a big celebration on Chinese New Year's Day. Such integration is necessary for the many American families whose traditions are rooted in different cultures.

Li, like Irene and John and so many others taking the family gamble, risked changing her ideas about family and tradition in order to adapt to a new situation. She was not ready to abandon entirely the rich culture of her native land; nor was she willing to raise her child outside the American culture into which the baby had been born. The compromise she decided on enabled her family to move forward with their lives, secure in knowing they could hold on to some of her mother's family traditions and blend them with the new. Li could merge two opposing ideas, keeping her mother both absent and present. And that is the goal for those experiencing ambiguous loss.

≻ *7* ≺

The Turning Point

IN THE GREEK LANGUAGE, CRISIS MEANS TURNING POINT. So it is with ambiguous loss. At some point, most people suffering uncertain loss will hit bottom and then, suddenly or after a long time, shift their perceptions about the status of a family member who is physically or psychologically absent. New information will emerge or one person in the family will get tired of the status quo and decide to do something different.[1] Because change may break family rules and traditions, everyone within the family is affected. But those who opt for change are no longer immobilized. As ambivalence and denial weaken, family members often come to accept that the ambiguous loss is here to stay. They begin to appraise their situation, make decisions, and take action. This is the turning point.

For the wives of missing American soldiers in Vietnam, the turning point came for many when they could no longer stay silent, as the military had recommended. They broke the rules and picketed at the Paris Peace Talks, where United States and North Vietnamese officials met after the fighting

106

stopped. They had been told to stay silent about their husbands' disappearance, which only increased their immobilization and feelings of helplessness. But some took risks, picketing the peace talks and speaking out about the missing men. Doing something, even if it broke the rules, was better than waiting and doing nothing.

Ambiguous loss makes us feel incompetent. It erodes our sense of mastery and destroys our belief in the world as a fair, orderly, and manageable place. But if we are to learn to cope with uncertainty, we must realize that there are differing views of the world, even when that world is less challenged by ambiguity. In 1989, when William F. Buckley mentioned a troubling statistic about overpopulation to Mother Teresa, she responded, "It's in God's hands."[2] Buckley grinned and asked her, "Are you sure?" These two people illustrate the extremes in how we approach problems. Buckley is typical of many of us who believe in mastering nature, whereas Mother Teresa represents an extraordinary spiritual acceptance. Both views are essential in learning to live with ambiguous loss.

If we are to turn the corner and cope with uncertain losses, we must first temper our hunger for mastery. This is the paradox. To regain a sense of mastery when there is ambiguity about a loved one's absence or presence, we must give up trying to find the perfect solution. We must redefine our relationship to the missing person. Most important, we must realize that the confusion we are experiencing is attributable to the ambiguity rather than to something we did—or neglected to do. Once we know the source of our helplessness, we are free to begin the coping process. We assess the situation, begin revising our perceptions of who is in the family

108 and on what basis, and gradually reconstruct family roles, rules, and rituals. We feel more in charge even though the ambiguity persists.

The elderly wife of a man with advanced Alzheimer's arrived at a research interview distraught. Her husband wanted sex all the time, she said, and this distressed her because he no longer even knew who she was. When interviewed a few months later, this same woman appeared serene. I asked her what had changed. She reported that one day a solution to her problem had suddenly occurred to her. She went into the bedroom, took off her wedding ring, and put it away in her jewelry box. After that, she said, she knew how to manage her husband's behavior. She no longer saw him as her husband but simply as someone she loved and would care for. Just as she had done with their children years ago, she set boundaries, moving him to a separate bedroom and directing his daily routines. The stress level for both patient and caregiver went down. On the day her husband died, two years later, she went to her jewelry box, took out her wedding ring, and placed it back on her finger. "Now I am really a widow," she said, "not just a widow waiting to happen."

This woman reached her turning point and regained control once she was able to label the ambiguity—in her words, she was "a widow waiting to happen." Knowing what she had lost (a husband) and what she still had (a human being she cared about) enabled her to manage the situation. By her own action, she became temporarily unmarried, transforming her role from wife to caretaker. With this perceptual shift, she no longer felt overwhelmed and helpless.

In my clinical work with caregiving families of people with

dementia and other chronic mental illnesses, I find that individuals are stimulated to change by different things. For people who are accustomed to having some control over their lives, insight appears to help; such people want to understand "why," to penetrate the deeper meaning of an experience before they risk doing something different. But for others, insight is gained experientially, not cognitively. For them, the family therapist Carl Whitaker was right when he said, "You only know what something is after you've gone past it." People have to experience a phenomenon before they can understand it. What is clear to me is that we as clinicians must be more sensitive to individual differences in ways of understanding a situation if we are to avoid creating the very resistance we sometimes attribute to the people we are trying to help.

For some people, mastery means controlling what is internal—perceptions, feelings, emotions, or memories—while for others it means controlling what is external—other people, a situation, or the environment. When a loved one is partially absent or present, few know what to do, so those who suffer, like the elderly woman who removed her wedding ring, must find their own solutions. Internal shifts are often linked to external control.

The first step a family therapist must take in helping people deal with their confusion and reach their own turning point is to label what they are experiencing as an ambiguous loss. In my own practice I often hear sighs of relief from people who are comforted to know not only that what they are feeling has a name, but also that they are not the only ones dealing with this kind of pain. They are comforted to learn that what they

110   are feeling is not their fault, and that their stress can be managed even if the ambiguity persists.

Nonetheless, something has to change. I tell family members that while feelings of confusion are normal with an ambiguous loss, maladaptations to that loss can cause problems in families. People may drink too much, eat or sleep too much—or too little—or they may become obstreperous in a desperate attempt to master a situation that defies their control. Once the problem of maladaption is identified, however, they can learn more functional ways of coping with their particular ambiguous loss. Once they understand *why* they are stuck, and that it isn't their fault, they are often more willing to change. At this point, I suggest family meetings.[3]

For the first of four to six family meetings, I gather together in one room everyone who is considered "family." A mixture of males and females from different generations is ideal because they will often express different but important viewpoints. Family members who have moved far away are often included via speaker phone. The hope is that these family meetings will become a regular occurrence once I am no longer working with the family. Note that the word "meeting" is used rather than "therapy." I avoid the latter term because in cases of ambiguous loss, it is the situation, not the family, that is sick.

My goal in working with the family is for all members to become aware of one another's interpretations of the experience of ambiguous loss, and to determine if there is some measure of agreement about how they see the situation. If there is strong disagreement in their perceptions of whether the family member in question is absent or present, here or gone, my main task in the first session is to verify that differing views are normal when there is an ambiguous loss in the family. I emphasize the importance of hearing and respecting one another's perceptions in order to maintain close relationships during a period of ambiguity.

As the family meets and talks together in the next few sessions, conflict and disagreements invariably occur, and there is often a tendency to want to stop meeting. I encourage family members to continue, since this is their chance to learn how to negotiate and problem-solve together in spite of their distressing ambiguous loss. Coping never happens in a vacuum; loved ones and friends can provide a mirror for one another's perceptions and behaviors, so that through continued discussions, what is irretrievably lost—and what is not—becomes clearer to everyone. People are no longer immobilized; they can mourn.

Coming together and talking allows a necessary exchange of information among the healthy family members, but what about the patient? In cases of chronic illness, the sick family member is also confused and distressed. Terminally ill patients say that they know they are slipping away and wonder if they are still valued, still a part of the family. They, too, feel guilt and shame as a result of their inability to be fully present.

Thus I think it is important to include the patient in at least some of the family meetings. Even Alzheimer's patients can detect when the family is acting as if they are already gone, and they, too, need an opportunity to express themselves. One patient, described by his family (in his presence) as capable of talking only nonsense, protested and told us that he was sure his wife was planning to divorce him. His wife said we shouldn't listen to him because he no

112   longer made sense, but in fact, she was planning to institutionalize him.

This family, which struggled with addiction issues on top of Alzheimer's, used the meetings to clear up, for themselves and for the patient, whether he was in or out of the family. In this case, it turned out he was out. His children were busy and his wife wanted her freedom so she could continue to gamble. Although there was no divorce, his detachment from the family was real. The patient is still living, and because his dementia has not deepened, he helps other patients in the institution that he now calls home.

During our meetings, I encourage family members to gather as much information as they can about their specific ambiguous loss. I encourage them to be aggressive, to insist on getting even professional literature since almost every family these days has someone in it who can translate technical information for the rest of the family. Families coping with an illness can find journals in libraries, write letters to request consultations with specialists, and contact other families with similar experiences. Families dealing with a physical loss can contact the police, surf the Internet, hire detectives, form networks of those suffering a similar loss, and fight to change laws. If the situation involves a soldier who has disappeared, loved ones can journey to distant places, build memorials, visit museums and cemeteries, or return to the killing fields. The act of seeking information eases the stress of ambiguity. Once that process is exhausted and no more information is available, that, too, becomes information, and helps people conclude, "We have done all that we can."

It is also very important for family members attending the meetings to learn to recognize their emotions—anger, pain,

sadness, shame, guilt, joy, relief, or terror. Rules from families of origin as well as the larger society often influence which
emotions are permissible for men and women and for girls
and boys, and how the expression of those feelings might
manifest itself. Some people pray, some drink or otherwise
sedate themselves; others connect with friends or family for
warmth and support; still others look to technology for help,
using the Internet to obtain information and to find help. In
family meetings, I help everyone to express their feelings in
nondestructive ways, and ask for tolerance for one another's
differences.

From my perspective, this is most effectively accomplished
experientially. I ask family members to tell stories about how
they celebrate special holidays and family rituals, stories
about how their lives have changed since the ambiguous loss,
and stories of how they survive and overcome difficulties.
They are encouraged to review photos, videos, mementos,
letters, and diaries as well as other symbols of the absent
person. Collectively and through the use of narratives, family
members begin to recognize and grieve what has been lost;
but at the same time, they become clearer about which aspects of their loved one are still present. Sometimes there are
surprising revelations or bitter disagreements during our conversations, but most often, with coaching, the family members work it out. If not, I ask them if they would like to shift
to more traditional family therapy in order to work on
specific issues. In the case of the family who closed out the
Alzheimer's patient, they were not willing to do this; nor were
they willing to seek treatment for their addictions. Change
was too frightening for them, so instead they excluded the
patient from their family.

114   Family meetings are a useful tool for coping with present and future ambiguous losses. I encourage families to make such meetings a part of their lives together because as people grow older and health status shifts, questions of who is in charge, who performs which roles, which rules need to change, and how family rituals and celebrations are to be observed and adapted invariably arise. Continuous restructuring is essential for any family to function and survive over time, but it is particularly important under the added stress of ambiguous loss.

As a therapist dealing with unresolved grief, I avoid telling people that there is just one "right" way to cope with uncertainty. What I may see as a problematic coping strategy may not be viewed as such by the family, particularly if their beliefs, socialization of gender and generational roles, and cultural values do not define it negatively. Change in such families will be resisted until their views are heard nonjudgmentally.[4] Certainly if a family member is in danger I must intervene, but my primary task is to listen, coach, stimulate, or question, and remind myself not to impede the process of brainstorming that will ultimately help the family reach a turning point.

When I was working with families caring for Alzheimer's patients, someone from my team would ask a question, after which the family members would take over, serving as sounding boards and mirrors for one another. Sometimes priests, rabbis, schoolteachers, neighbors, or friends would be asked to join a family meeting, for it is often helpful to see how the family's own community views the ambiguous loss. Opening up the discussion even further, some families would meet with others experiencing similar losses in order to see how they learned to cope.

As I work with families who are just beginning the process of coping with an ambiguous loss, I try to reinforce any behaviors that enhance physical activity and interaction with other human beings, because active coping behaviors are considered more functional than passive ones. But passivity, at times, is also a necessary part of the healing process. Family members need to communicate with one another about their loss, but they also need to rest—even escape—now and then in order to tolerate long-term ambiguous loss. Respite is essential and no one should feel guilty for taking it. If people are to avoid becoming depressed or melancholy after long periods of tending to a loved one's needs, they must learn to take care of themselves. In such cases I recommend that family members do something, anything, to become more active again, physically and socially.

I also encourage families to use humor as a coping mechanism. Humor is an important adaptive response to adversity. Some, however, find it disrespectful to be humorous or to play in the presence of suffering individuals or families. Certainly, it is difficult to find something humorous in ambiguous losses that are tragic and catastrophic. Yet play is a powerful interpersonal tool, and its therapeutic effects have been well proven.

Being together and laughing, even for a few minutes, is healthy. Often in the family meetings people will tell stories—funny ones—about their tendencies to settle the ambiguity by prematurely closing out their loved one or by denying that anything is wrong. By laughing at themselves, they relieve stress for the whole group. While their stories are

116   often bittersweet, laughter brings balance to their heavy chore of coping and grieving in spite of ambiguity. If we can laugh about our propensity for absolute solutions, then we can begin to loosen up and see other options.

My research with families coping with dementia has shown that both mastery and a spiritual acceptance of the situation are highly functional for caregiving families as they live with the ambiguous loss of Alzheimer's disease. Indeed, those who use only mastery manifest the most anxiety and depression. This is true for other ambiguous losses as well. I recall the words of my grandmother Sophie, who in her letters to my father continually reflected her use of both mastery and spiritual acceptance. When she couldn't solve a problem, she would write, "Always trust in God." But she also wrote poetically about mastery. "Learn to build hearth and home. Always keep your head high no matter what menace comes your way." Her powers for coping with life came from a combination of spirituality and mastery, as was the case with the Anishinabe women I interviewed in Minnesota. From those women I also learned that a terminal illness is less distressful when it is attributed to the natural cycle of life rather than to failure. The secret to coping with the pain of an uncertain loss, regardless of culture or personal beliefs, is to avoid feeling helpless. This is accomplished by working to change what we can and accepting what we cannot.

I am reminded of a Russian film I once saw about an old woman who is bedridden and paralyzed except for one finger, which is tied to a string that leads to a loud bell. Every time she moves her little finger, the bell reverberates throughout the household. This patient, although incapacitated, con-

trols the destiny of the entire family. They are prisoners of her
bell. In order for families to live with chronically ill persons in
the household, *both* patient and family must strike a balance
between mastery and acceptance. Only then will they be able
to move beyond the pain of long-term ambiguity.

≍ 8 ≍

Making Sense out of Ambiguity

> Loss wasn't—mustn't be, couldn't be—an end in itself. It had
> to mean something. But finding out its meaning was like
> scaling a gigantic wall. Was it there just so I could get over it?
> —Susanna Tamaro, *Follow Your Heart*

THE LAST AND MOST DIFFICULT STEP IN RESOLVING ANY
loss is to make sense of it. In the case of ambiguous loss,
gaining meaning is even more difficult than in an ordinary
loss, because the grief itself remains unresolved. But if we
cannot make sense out of ambiguity, nothing really changes.
We merely endure.

Maintaining hope in the face of long-term ambiguity requires ceaseless effort, bringing to mind the story of Sisyphus.[1] The gods condemn Sisyphus to an eternity of
laboriously rolling a rock to the top of a mountain. When he
finally reaches the top, the boulder rolls back down and
Sisyphus has to start all over again. There was no more
dreadful punishment, the gods thought, than hopeless labor.

The story is tragic only because Sisyphus is aware that
there is no hope of his succeeding. The problem he faces can

never be solved. Such ceaseless labor is precisely what people   **119**
with ambiguous loss face—people like the elderly woman
who tenderly cares for a husband who no longer remembers
her; the mother who ceaselessly searches for a missing child;
the sister of a missing soldier who relentlessly presses the
government to keep searching; and the friends who work
around the clock to care for an AIDS patient who is dying.
Unlike Sisyphus, however, those suffering unresolved grief
can still cling to hope. The goal for families is to find some
way to change even though the ambiguity remains. This is yet
another paradox—to transform a situation that won't
change.

Many people succeed. Indeed, many in my research and
clinical work are able to see some hope in their ambiguous
loss. It is not the situation that changes but what they hope
for. When an illness won't go away, people creatively find
hope in other ways—in doing their best to manage the illness,
in helping others who are experiencing the same pain, or in
finding ways to prevent others from having the same experience. With surprising ingenuity, people infuse what looks like
a tragic situation with hope. Parents of missing children lobby
lawmakers and are successful in having laws changed to be
more protective of children; they create international computer networks so that photographs of missing children can
be transmitted nationally and globally in real time. Family
members of the mentally or physically ill work to change laws
and form national alliances that influence how health care
workers practice and how much money the government allo-
cates to research for catastrophic illnesses. People use their
powers of mastery to make changes, not always to alter the
tragedy of their own loss, but to help others who might be

suffering a similar loss in the future. If the world is unjust for having caused their ambiguous loss, they resolve to make meaning out of the chaos by lowering the risks of such loss for others.

From my own research and clinical observations, as well as the research of others, I have found that several factors influence how families gain meaning from ambiguous losses. The first factor is the family of origin and early social experiences. Families are the first place we learn about the rules, roles, and rituals for making sense out of loss. As I work with couples and families, I inquire about how their families worked. Were they permitted to express sad feelings? Were only women and girls expected to care for the frail and the dying? Were men and boys expected to remain stoic? Were family rituals and celebrations ever altered, and if so, why? Who in their family was known to be able to tolerate not having the answer to a problem? What did they think it was that allowed that person to tolerate ambiguity—personality, gender, age, life experience, or religious beliefs? These questions help me to gain an impression of how people have been taught to deal with situations that make no sense.

Because rituals and celebrations often reveal a lot about a family, I see these events as sources for clues about a family's tolerance for ambiguity. I ask couples and families about their special events—holiday celebrations, rituals of birth, adulthood, marriage, and death, as well as celebrations of achievement such as graduations and other recognition ceremonies. In order to determine who is in the family, I ask who is invited to these events and who is not. I also ask who performs which roles as well as what the rules are, implicit and explicit, for changing family rituals and celebrations. Centering the family discussions on such memorable events is especially useful because it helps them find meaning in their unclear loss.

The Olson family always met every November in the family home for Thanksgiving. Three generations would gather around a large dining-room table bedecked with food and heirloom china. At the head of the table would sit Mr. Olson, beloved father and grandfather. Once the turkey was brought in on a huge platter from the kitchen, the ceremony would begin. The family would sit down and all eyes would be on Mr. Olson as he prepared to carve the twenty-pound turkey. Everyone loved this moment. But this year, something was wrong. Mr. Olson was making a mess out of the turkey. As he was attempting to carve it, the bird suddenly and ceremoniously slid off the platter onto the tablecloth and then onto the floor. Silence. The first to speak was Mrs. Olson, who expressed concern about the stains on the rug and on the antique tablecloth. But everyone, including Mr. Olson, was painfully embarrassed because he could no longer perform this holiday ritual as he used to, with dignity and precision. They all knew the doctors had diagnosed Alzheimer's disease, but since the diagnosis was not certain, they denied its possibility. But at Thanksgiving they all saw his failing abilities and had to accept that he was changing. The next year, Mrs. Olson suggested that they skip the family Thanksgiving dinner to save the family and Grandfather the embarrassment of his no longer being able to carve the turkey.

This pattern of canceling the celebration instead of altering it is a common response in families with ambiguous loss. Once these families begin communicating in family sessions, however, some of them, usually the young children, push for the continuation of tradition. I then ask the family to brain-

122   storm about how they might continue the celebration in a revised way, in this case, so as to avoid embarrassment but not lose the meaning of the event. Could someone else take Grandfather's place? Could Grandmother sit at the head of the table and carve the turkey? Could the eldest son or daughter perform this role? No. In the Olson family, no one wanted to displace this cherished man from his spot at the head of the table. Then someone came up with a different idea: "Let's leave everything exactly the way it has been, but change one thing. Someone can carve the turkey in the kitchen, and then bring it in and place it in front of Grandpa, who will still be sitting at the head of the table. Those sitting near him can help serve." A simple idea, yet so profound in its meaning.

This family, unaccustomed to spontaneity and flexibility, had earlier not thought about adaptation and change. They were initially inclined to cancel the ritual dinner because of the patriarch's deteriorating health. Their first shift was to adopt the suggestion that Grandfather be handed an already-carved turkey, but as the dementia deepened—and as gender roles became more flexible—Mrs. Olson took over at the head of the Thanksgiving table, since she was now the head of the family. Grandfather sat at her side, now more relaxed than when he was still trying to perform a role he could no longer manage. Clearly, family celebrations and rituals do not have to be discontinued just because there is an ambiguous loss, but the people involved must discover what their loss means to them before they can alter their family traditions.

People who can accept a situation without having to master it often find it easier to be spontaneous and flexible about changing long-standing patterns and traditions. But my work has taught me that everyone, no matter the age, can change if 123 they want to; and that they are relieved to learn they can revise cherished family traditions instead of giving them up altogether.

Families attempting to make meaning out of ambiguous loss are also influenced by their spirituality. In research interviews and in my clinical work, people often tell me they find peace and strength in their spiritual beliefs. An adult son and daughter from one family I interviewed came to a family session because they were afraid that the stress their eighty-year-old mother was experiencing would kill her before their father died from his dementia. Both son and daughter were executives in large firms. They were fidgety, talked rapidly, and kept looking at their mother and then at their watches.

Meanwhile, Mother sat serenely. She did not look distressed, though her children did. Son said, "Mother, we have to do something. You have to be so stressed with all the work you're doing to take care of Dad." "But I am not," she responded. "I have God to help and protect me as I do the work." Her daughter looked disgusted. "But, Mother, you *have* to be stressed!"

What I saw was adult children who were full of anxiety and stress, but an elderly mother who was content with her lot. Indeed, her burden was heavy, but she did not perceive it as such. The situation appeared to take a greater toll on her children, who were not even helping with the caregiving.

I shared what I saw as I talked with the family. For the next few meetings, the children moved toward recognizing that their own anxiety was heightened by their lack of participation in the family at this time. We talked about how their mother's work could become more of a team effort. Even

124 though they had busy careers, they talked with their mother about what they could do to help. One took charge of the paperwork, which was considerable, and the other agreed to take charge of finding some respite or day care so that their mother could have at least one afternoon off each week. In the end, the son and daughter even laughed a little about the fact that the stress was their problem even more than their mother's. The elderly woman smiled knowingly, adding, "I know God is helping me, but I like it that you help, too."

The Anishinabe women in northern Minnesota also turned to spirituality in their acceptance of an elder's dementia. Ruby said, "I was always taught that things happen for reasons, and my aunt being sick, there was a reason that God had her be sick, and that's the only way I can justify it." Another woman said, "What I think is that God does not give you more than you can deal with . . . And I think that everything that is happening is sort of happening in a way that every time I do something, it leads me to something else . . . I look at Mom almost the same darn way [as I do my children and grandchildren]. It's like the old story they tell, you crawl into this world and then back out." With Alzheimer's, the circle of life was completed, as a third woman explained: "[My mother] came in as a small child; it's like this whole circle and she's winding down and just going back in . . . she became a little child again."[2] Although people experiencing ambiguous losses have very different beliefs about spirituality and God, what unites them is their ability to find some meaning in their situation, uncertain as it is.

Another factor influencing how people make sense out of ambiguous loss is their way of thinking. Are they optimistic or pessimistic? The caregiving wife of a man who had become incontinent said, "He is just getting back at me for all the times I made him mad! He'll kill me yet!" She interpreted her caregiving duties in the worst possible light. Another woman with a similar situation said, "I have been given one last chance to show how much I love my husband. I know I can do this." Not surprisingly, with her more optimistic assessment, the second woman's depressive symptoms were fewer and her health was better than the first woman's. These two caregivers required vastly different methods of intervention and support because of their ways of processing information. The optimist saw the jar as half full; the pessimist saw it as half empty.

The psychologist Martin Seligman calls such optimism and pessimism "habits of thinking."[3] He explains that pessimists "tend to believe bad events will last a long time, will undermine everything they do, and are their own fault. The optimists, who are confronted with the same hard knocks . . . tend to believe defeat is just a temporary setback, that its causes are confined to this one case." Optimists believe that being unable to solve a problem is the result of outside circumstances or bad luck rather than something they did. People who tend to think optimistically are, according to Seligman, unfazed by defeat. When confronted by a bad situation, they simply see it as a challenge and try harder.

As long as there is optimism and hope, continuing to work on a relationship with someone who is slowly dying can be a kind of victory, as can continuing to work on a relationship with a divorced mate who cooperates in parenting the children, or letting kids come back home after they leave, knowing they will leave again, or continuing to search for a missing parent or child. This is what human beings do—we keep on

126   pushing the rock up the hill. If we do it with optimism, there is no absurdity in perseverance.

Finally, people's view of how the world works influences how they find meaning in ambiguous loss. Viewing the world logically, as a fair and just place, can stand in the way of tolerating ambiguous loss. People who see the world this way feel that we get what we deserve. That is, if we work hard and are moral, we will be successful and happy. The other side of this view, however, is rife with judgment and blame: if people have troubles, it is their own fault. They or their families must have been incompetent, lazy, or immoral, and thus they are being justly punished. The problem with this world view, of course, is that bad things also happen to good people. Mental and physical illnesses and natural disasters are not any one person's fault. Yet such external events can lead to severe losses in families. Finding blame is rarely helpful.

If we ask the fundamental question, "Why did this happen?" we must be prepared to look beyond the neat equations of cause and effect and learn to live with uncertainty. We cannot know for sure why bad things happen to good people, but we do know that *not* everything that happens is a result of our actions. Learning to let go of cause-and-effect thinking is difficult because most of us have been trained to view the world as a rational place: Mother lost her mind because she didn't eat right; a boy was kidnapped because his parents let him go to the store; a husband drinks because his wife nags. I hear such linear views all the time in my practice, and they result from the inherent need to find fault. People cling to the view that the world is *always* just, for if it is not, then there is no way for them to control the randomness of their own losses. And this is a frightening thought for many.

In Jane Smiley's *One Thousand Acres,* the character of
Rose illustrates the belief in a just world in a conversation
with her sister: "Ginny, I know what I think because I've
thought about it for a long time. I thought about it in the
hospital, after the operation. You know, Mommy dying, and
Daddy, and Pete being such a mean drunk, and having to
send the girls away, and then losing a part of my own body on
top of it all. In the face of that, if there aren't some rules, then
what is there? There's got to be something, order, rightness.
Justice, for God's sake."[4]

The need to place blame is common in people facing a loss
or other traumatic experience. A soldier who had been a
prisoner of war told me that it had taken him a long time to
make sense out of his capture. I asked him to explain. He said
at first he had thought it was his fault, that he hadn't run fast
enough to catch the helicopter, that he hadn't been fit enough.
But after being in captivity for a time, he said, his blame had
shifted. "To whom?" I asked. "To politicians," he said. His
anger, no longer so deeply aimed at himself but now attributed to an external cause, changed the meaning of his capture, thereby aiding his and his family's recovery from the
ordeal.

Those who don't blame themselves or others will often
attribute their misfortune to bad luck. This is a more functional approach to ambiguous loss than is self-blame. Indeed,
attributing the uncertainty surrounding a loss to randomness
is in itself a way of making sense of it. We did everything
right, but it just happened. The knowledge that we can't
always know why things happen is an answer in itself.

Determining that ambiguous loss is often caused by an
external force and not one's own shortcomings is at the same

128   time tragic and freeing. The loss is not resolved as a result, but many people are able to find meaning in their tragedy. Recall the story of Betty and Kenny Klein, whose three sons disappeared. Their initial assumption was that they might have been bad parents. But when Betty subsequently became pregnant again, she interpreted their having more children as an affirmation from God that they were good parents: "He was giving us children back, not ever to replace the three that were gone, because you can't, but proving to us, in a way, I thought, that we were good parents anyway." She even came to believe that her loss held some meaning for other parents: "I thought, well, maybe other mothers will look at their children and hold them a little bit closer, you know, because of it. I'm sure there [were] a lot of parents that took their children in their arms, you know, when that happened to our children. I'm sure there [were]."[5] As I listened with admiration to this woman in her sunny home, I was reminded of a line by Carl Jung: "Meaning makes a great many things endurable—perhaps everything."[6]

Self-blame is dysfunctional because it prevents us from moving on with our lives. If we can't forgive ourselves—or others—we ruminate about the past; there is no closure. We cannot grieve. The most public experiment minimizing blame in order to heal in the wake of ambiguous loss is now taking place in South Africa.[7]

After decades of terror, there is no documentation in South Africa of the many victims who were lost in the struggle for freedom. A Truth and Reconciliation Commission has been formed by the new government headed by President Nelson Mandela. Leading the commission is Bishop Desmond Tutu, who made an unprecedented call for public testimony in exchange for amnesty for most perpetrators and facts for most victims' families. It works this way: a mother tells her story about her missing son; the perpetrator then explains how, when, and where he tortured and murdered her son. Piecing together the facts, she gets a more complete story of what happened and whether her boy is really dead. Officials gamble that the perpetrator's public confession and the victim's telling the story of her missing child will lead to reconciliation between two enemies and ultimately societal healing. The premise is that the process of confessing and forgiving works. But I would add that the process also works because it gives the families as much information as possible about their missing loved ones. Of course, there is no guarantee that the perpetrators will be sincere in their confessions, given that the reward of amnesty over punishment is tempting. Perhaps the people of South Africa—and any other country in which people have disappeared without verification of death—can come to terms with their ambiguous losses even though they know the solution will not be perfect. I think of the many missing children in this world and how clear information, even from a perpetrator, would help so many of their families to bring closure to a devastating loss. Knowing for sure what happened to a missing child, whether that child is alive—or, if dead, where the body is—would for many parents be worth granting amnesty. For many, information verifying a loss is worth even more than retaliation. Thus, we must watch the South African experiment closely, for if it works, it could provide a unique way to clear up ambiguous losses on a national scale after major catastrophes such as wars.

Storytelling has always been a way to find meaning about loss. Many South Africans grew up hearing old tribal stories

130   that were often about victims, victimizers, and forgiveness; Native Americans told stories to heal. The current revival of narrative analysis is just another testimony to the usefulness of storytelling in making sense of our losses.[8] Maybe those of us trained in positivist traditions should listen more carefully to people's stories in order to hear new questions, new answers, and, more important, new meanings that families have about living with losses they can't resolve. In doing so, we together find meaning in the chaos.

Families tell me that old stories filled with rituals, symbols, and metaphors are helpful when they are struggling to make sense of an ambiguous loss. One family of an Alzheimer's patient saw their varying perceptions as similar to a 1920s Rashomon tale by the Japanese writer Akutagawa. In that story, witnesses to a crime that took place in a grove tell conflicting accounts of what happened.[9] Each witness tells what he or she saw, and as with present-day witnesses, their stories are not the same. All have different perceptions of what happened, and all believe their own story to be the truth. This tale reminds families that the absence and presence of a loved one is relative. They learn that differing interpretations will occur among family members, and that it is not necessary to seek perfect symmetry in their understanding of the loss.

Another story surfaced as I was interviewing the wives of missing pilots. Several of the women often referred to Antoine de Saint-Exupéry's *The Little Prince*. They said it helped them to make sense out of their husbands' disappearance. I had not read the book, thinking it was for children, but I turned to it immediately after speaking with the women. It became apparent right away why the story was helpful. Not

only was the Little Prince a downed pilot, but the story is full 131
of meaning about the ambiguity of absence and presence, as
well as the real matters of consequence.

The Prince teaches the fox that being tamed is very important in life; he stresses that it is vital to make connections. At
first, the fox resists being tamed by the Prince, but then he
gives in, knowing the risk:

> If you tame me, it will be as if the sun came to shine on my life.
> I shall know the sound of a step that will be different from all
> the others. Other steps send me hurrying back underneath the
> ground. Yours will call me, like music, out of my burrow. And
> then look: you see the grain-fields down yonder? I do not eat
> bread. Wheat is of no use to me. The wheat fields have nothing
> to say to me. And that is sad. But you have hair that is the color
> of gold. Think how wonderful that will be when you have
> tamed me! The grain, which is also golden, will bring me back
> the thought of you. And I shall love to listen to the wind in the
> wheat.[10]

Being tamed, or having a close relationship, makes us
vulnerable to loss, but the risk is worth it. Every time we
metaphorically look at the wheat fields or the stars, we remember our loved one; he or she is with us at that moment.
"It has done me good," said the fox, "because of the color of
the wheat fields."[11] With ambiguous loss it is essential that we
struggle to understand even what doesn't make sense.

The process of comprehending and moving on when someone we love is physically or psychologically missing is immensely difficult. Stories help some people to make sense of
their situation. More than scientifically precise answers,
metaphors and symbols allow us to transcend the immediate
situation and find meaning in our loss. Often when we step

134   Becoming aware that someone we care about is neither here nor there is tragic. But at the same time, ambiguous loss can, in spite of high stress, produce some good. In the confusion and lack of rigidity lie opportunities for creativity and new ways of being that have some purpose and a chance for growth.

The Pulleyblank family experienced eight years of agony watching a father slip away from Lou Gehrig's disease; he became increasingly paralyzed until he could only blink his eyes. Early in the illness, both parents courageously showed their children how to live to the fullest with what was left of their time together. They talked about what was happening and struggled together to try to understand what it all meant. With the help of friends and family they often pushed the bounds of their limited life by taking Ron out into the world in his wheelchair attached to a ventilator—to the symphony, the ocean, and to Yosemite to see the mountains he once climbed. The family became experts at living with ambiguity, for though the disease was terminal, its course was unpredictable. Years later, Ellen Pulleyblank, a therapist herself, tells me that among the hard lessons she learned during her husband's illness was that she must stop expecting rational explanations for the unexplainable; let go of trying to control the uncontrollable; and witness the suffering of another by staying present and doing only what is possible. She had never thought of herself as the kind of person who needed help, but she admits that "without the help that I learned to ask for and generously receive, we would never have been able to learn to live with such adversity."[2]

After such experiences with ambiguity, family members are often better able to explore unknown territory in many other areas of life—they may take chances in their careers, try 135 white water rafting, travel on their own in foreign countries, even get married. They are capable of taking risks because they have learned to live with uncertainty.

Ambiguous loss is devastating and can have lasting traumatic effects. But with support and resilience some people use the experience to learn how to live in difficult circumstances throughout life, balancing the ability to grieve what was lost with the recognition of what is still possible.

Ambiguity can make people less dependent on stability and more comfortable with spontaneity and change. Reaching this point is frightening, however, especially for those who are accustomed to being in charge. With ambiguous loss, the task is to let go, to risk moving forward, even when we do not know exactly where we are going. We move to keep from freezing in place or becoming comfortably static; and we do this with actions that are life-enhancing.

Both loss and ambiguity are core elements of the human experience, so it is not surprising that they often merge as *ambiguous loss*. The absence of certainty contains an element of advantage over more ordinary loss because one is free to hope for a positive outcome. Viktor Frankl, in his account of life in a Nazi concentration camp, called this "tragic optimism."[3] Some older families I interviewed called it "the silver lining." Gilda Radner called it "delicious ambiguity."

The thirty-nine-year-old Radner, who was battling advanced ovarian cancer, hoped to end her book documenting her illness with news of recovery, but instead ends with a homage to ambiguity: "Now I've learned, the hard way, that some poems don't rhyme, and some stories don't have a clear beginning, middle and end . . . Like my life, this book is about

136   not knowing, having to change, taking the moment and making the best of it, without knowing what's going to happen next. Delicious ambiguity . . . I may never be able to control the fear and the panic, but I have learned to control how I live each day."[4] She died in 1986.

Family members often struggle with ambiguity even longer than the patient because those left behind must continue to make some sense out of their loss. Their task is to risk moving forward in the fog. Gradually, they regain some sense of mastery and are able to make decisions and cope. They often do something purposeful to give meaning to their tragic loss. Radner's husband, the actor Gene Wilder, established Gilda's Club, a support community in New York City for cancer patients and their families.

Many mates and family members, like Wilder, find the information and support they desperately need by participating in groups with other people who are experiencing the same loss. But support groups are not the only source of optimism. Coping strategies will vary from person to person. Some people find hope in religion, others in the arts; still others say that priests, rabbis, ministers, shamans, and even artists are simply illusion sustainers who persuade us that "hope is up ahead."[5] What is important is that therapists, friends, and community members recognize that those suffering ambiguous losses will have their own, unique ways of functioning amid blatant contradictions in a loved one's absence or presence. It is our job to support their efforts to find meaning in their loss—provided that their solutions are safe—regardless of where that may lead.

We can learn about coping with uncertainty by paying attention to the daily contradictions in contemporary family life as well as to the major contradictions from catastrophic illness or traumatic events. Becoming comfortable with ambiguous loss day to day will help prepare us for more serious ambiguity. Many of us, for example, deal with ambiguity and ambivalence in that increasingly blurred place between providing and parenting. In balancing the demands of work and family, a parent is both absent and present for the children. At times of important family celebrations, this confusion can be especially stressful.

Congresswoman Patricia Schroeder, who raised two children while serving in the U.S. House of Representatives, explained how she turned a negative ambiguity into a positive one by blending the realities of her private and public lives for her child's birthday party. "The institution tends to elect people to be its leaders who don't have a life, and they really don't know what family friendly means," she said, so she told House Speaker Tip O'Neil, "You can keep us late, but I get your dining room, and you can tell the Capitol police that when a clown comes in and ten five-year-olds, to get ready." The Speaker acquiesced, and her child's birthday party was held in his dining room. In spite of a chaotic political life, this mother transformed the ambiguity of her absence and presence in a way that benefited her children and at the same time did not affect her work. Family rituals were not sacrificed because of her work demands. The celebration changed in location, but it still took place and she was present at the party. In this case, the ambiguity was creatively revised into a positive experience.[6]

Absent and busy parents are not the only source of ambiguous loss in everyday life. Sophisticated technology now prolongs life after illness or brain injury; it complicates birth

138   by increasing the presence of shadow-parents resulting from artificial insemination, test tube conceptions, and host mothers. Adoptive families are also on the rise, and the extended family, long the favorite of new immigrants and migrants for economic reasons, is now becoming more common in middle-class homes, with both parents employed outside the home and adult children never leaving.

Sometimes the prevalence of ambiguity in contemporary life can be amusing, reaching even into people's spiritual life. In the Yokohma Chuo cemetery in Tokyo, a mechanical Buddhist priest with robotic blinking eyes and moving mouth now chants sutras each morning for the recently dead. The question is: Is a priest absent or present?

Although our longing for certainty is normal, it is also natural never to find it. As technology is increasingly able to mimic or conceive life as well as to extend it, as family disruptions mount, and as everyday work and family life continue to confuse absence and presence, the phenomenon of ambiguous loss in families will grow dramatically, making it even more vital that we learn to live as positively as possible with the stress of not knowing. In the end, what is needed is not absolute clarity, but rather an acknowledgment of ambiguous losses.

At some level we all wrestle with the paradox of human connections: the absent as present and the present as absent. Today, people are increasingly expected to take care of slowly dying loved ones. Still others are expected to care for themselves when family members are taken by earthquakes, floods, volcanoes, fires, or predators—their bodies never to be found. The grief in such cases is not resolvable in the usual way, and unless we confront the loss, the commonplace longing for loved ones who are, for whatever reason, **139** unreachable takes over our lives and prevents us from moving on.

And that brings me full circle. My task as a researcher and family therapist is to help individuals, couples, and families manage the stress of living with ambiguous losses. While doing this work, I could not help reflecting on my own family. I began to see my own experiences in a clearer light. In mid-summer of 1990, I drove back to my hometown in southern Wisconsin to be with an old and wonderful father who was dying. His body had simply worn out, but his mind was as clear as ever. We had always had good discussions, and it was the same now in the hospital. We talked about the crumbling of the Berlin Wall and other issues in the news, such as flag-burning. And we talked about death—his death. He said he had had a good life and was ready to die. He asked me to look out for my mother and not to forget him. Neither was difficult to promise.

Because the nurse said my father's condition was stable that night, I left the hospital knowing that we had a little more time. I slept in my mother's tidy house under a bedspread made of thousands of stitches from Grandmother Elsbeth's knitting needles. The yarn formed a spread of sculpted flowers and leaves in rich ivory, the crowning project of her handwork, an activity prescribed as therapy for her homesickness by a wise country doctor. He had seen so many Swiss immigrants in the community with somatic illness and depression that he started what we today would call a psychoeducational group.[7] Elsbeth's newfound project soon gave meaning to her days. Not only was she good at knitting, but the feel of the yarn connected her to her home in Switzerland,

140 where she had worked in a textile-weaving factory. As I lay under this symbol of my grandmother's "therapy" for homesickness and ambiguous loss, I was kept warm on those anxious nights as I awaited my father's death.

He lingered for another few months, but he was realistic about his condition. "I could die anytime. That's life at my age," he said. But then he added, with the hint of a twinkle in his eye, "They just gave me a woman doctor. Just looking at her makes me feel better." I smiled, too. He was at that moment again the father I knew, always the artist with an eye for things beautiful.

My father's heart failed in late October, just before his eighty-seventh birthday. His death was what grief experts call "normative," meaning it occurred at an old age, when it could be expected. Yet I will not forget the agony of those last few months. He was here—I could touch him—but he was clearly leaving. Shades of gray, I thought. Nothing was clear. I knew then that there was a measure of ambiguity even in an expected and timely death. And for the first time, I personally felt the positive side of ambiguous loss—it allowed me time to say goodbye. Not every death allows that benefit.

The dilemma for all of us is to bring clarity to an ambiguous situation. Failing that, and we will in most cases, the critical question is how to live with ambiguous loss. For each of us, the answer will be different. But the answers are less critical than the questions.

Notes

Acknowledgments

Notes

1. Frozen Grief

1. Here the term "ambiguous loss" is limited to personal relationships. Psychiatrists write about ambivalence and sociologists write about boundary permeability and role confusion, but none of these terms captures what I mean by ambiguous loss.

2. As early as 1970 Dr. Aaron Lazare found that unresolved grief was often a primary contributor to the distress of patients requesting mental health services. He briefly discusses uncertainties over a loss and the difficulties that follow. See A. Lazare, "The difference between sadness and depression," *Medical Insight,* 2 (1970): 23–31; and A. Lazare, *Outpatient Psychiatry: Diagnosis and Treatment,* 2nd ed. (Baltimore: Williams & Wilkins, 1989), pp. 381–397. See also K. J. Doka, ed., *Disenfranchised Grief* (New York: Lexington Books, 1989).

3. P. Boss, D. Pearce-McCall, and J. S. Greenberg, "Normative loss in mid-life families: Rural, urban, and gender differences," *Family Relations,* 36 (1987): 437–443.

4. I assessed depressive symptoms using the Zung Self-Rating Depression Scale and the Geriatric Depression Scale. See J. Yessavage and T. Brink, "The development and validation of a geriatric depression screening scale," *Journal of Psychiatric Research,* 17 (1) (1983): 37–49.

5. This qualitative research was funded by the University of Minnesota All-University Council on Aging, 1992–1993, P. Boss, principal investigator, "Caregiver Well-Being in Native American Families with Dementia." See P. Boss, L. Kaplan, and M. Gordon, "Accepting the circle of life," *Center for Urban and Regional Affairs Reporter,* 25, 3 (1995): 7–11.

144

2. Leaving without Goodbye

1. W. I. Thomas and F. Znaniecki, *The Polish Peasant in Europe and America*, 5 vols. (Boston: Badger, 1918–1920).

2. See *The Killing Fields*, ed. C. Riley and D. Niven (Santa Fe, N.M.: Twin Palms Publishers, 1996). One-quarter of the Cambodian population was killed under the regime. Seth Mydans in the *New York Times Book Review*, May 25, 1997, wrote: "Cambodia remains a suffering and unstable nation, a nation of 8 million victims of post-traumatic stress disorder. Virtually every Cambodian has lost family members to the Khmer Rouge terror; many watched as a mother or a brother was clubbed to death. Domestic abuse, random street crime and police brutality are currently endemic" (p. 21).

3. *Minneapolis Star Tribune*, March 30, 1997, p. A14.

4. D. Fravel, H. Grotevant, P. Boss, and R. McRoy, "Refining and extending the boundary ambiguity construct through application to families experiencing various levels of openness in adoption," *Journal of Marriage and the Family* (forthcoming).

5. H. Garland, *A Son of the Middle Border* (New York: Grosset & Dunlap with Macmillan, 1917), p. 238.

6. Ibid., p. 63. Garland was one of the first to address the issues of immigrant frontier women. Assigned the role of helping his mother and grandmother when he was young, he became aware of women's experience on the midwestern frontier.

7. W. D. Erikson wrote the history of St. Peter's in *The Great Charity: Minnesota's First Mental Hospital at St. Peter, Minn.* (self-published, 1991). While studying the period 1866 to 1991, he coincidentally found that his great-grandmother had been one of those women who sought asylum at the mental hospital. She spent the rest of her life there.

8. M. B. Theiler, *New Glarus' First Hundred Years* (Madison, Wis.: Campus Publishing Co., 1946), pp. 34–35.

9. G. Jacobsen-Marty, *Two for America* (Blanchardville, Wis.: Ski Printers, Inc., 1986).

10. Irish Folklore Department, manuscript 1411, University College, Dublin, Ireland.

11. Ellis Island Oral History Project, "Interview with B. Smith-Schneider," Ellis Island Immigration Museum (1986).

12. P. Boss, "The experience of immigration for the mother left behind: The use of qualitative feminist strategies to analyze letters from my Swiss grandmother to my father," *Families on the Move: Migration, Immigration, Emigration and Mobility,* special issue of *Marriage and Family Review,* 19 (3/4) (1993): 365–378.

13. S. Akhtar, "A third individuation: Immigration, identity, and the psychoanalytic process," *Journal of the American Psychoanalytic Association,* 43 (4) (1995): 1051–1084.

3. Goodbye without Leaving

1. *Losing It All* (HBO Production, Time-Warner Productions, Inc., 1991). Documentary film was written, edited, and produced by M. Meirendorf. P. Boss was a consultant.

2. P. Boss, W. Caron, J. Horbal, and J. Mortimer, "Predictors of depression in caregivers of dementia patients: Boundary ambiguity and mastery," *Family Process,* 29 (1990): 245–254.

3. *Losing It All.*

4. T. Sewell, *Mom's Quotes* (self-published, 1991).

5. T. Sewell, *I Am Not Fictional* (video in production).

6. R. M. Rilke, trans. S. Mitchell, *Letters to a Young Poet* (New York: Random House, 1984).

7. Willa Cather, *My Ántonia* (Boston: Houghton Mifflin Co., 1918), p. 127. The novelist Willa Cather wrote about immigrant girls who left home at early ages to work as "hired girls" in other people's homes.

4. Mixed Emotions

1. A. Lazare, *Outpatient Psychiatry: Diagnosis and Treatment,* 2nd ed. (Baltimore: Williams & Wilkins, 1989), pp. 389, 393; L. A. King and R. A. Emmons, "Psychological, physical, and interpersonal correlates of emotional expressiveness, conflict, and control," *European Journal of Personality,* 5 (1991): 131–150.

146   2. M. Robert and E. Barber, "Sociological ambivalence," in *Socio-logical Ambivalence and Other Essays* (New York: The Free Press, 1976), pp. 1–31. See also A. Weigert, *Mixed Emotions: Certain Steps toward Understanding Ambivalence* (Albany: State University of New York Press, 1991); McLain and A. Weigert, "Toward a phenome-nological sociology of family," in W. R. Burr, R. Hill, F. I. Nye, and I. L. Reiss, eds., *Contemporary Theories about the Family,* vol. 2 (New York: The Free Press, 1979), pp. 160–205. For more recent work, see K. Luescher and K. Pillemer, "Intergenerational ambivalence: A new approach to the study of parent-child relations in later life," *Journal of Marriage and the Family,* vol. 60 (1998), pp. 413–425.

3. *Good Morning America* (American Broadcasting Company, May 10, 1997).

4. A. M. Freedman, H. I. Kaplan, and B. J. Sadock, *Modern Synop-sis of Comprehensive Textbook of Psychiatry* (Baltimore: Williams & Wilkins, 1972), p. 105. The Electra Complex was thought of as the female version of the Oedipus Complex, with the addition of penis envy. The girl holds her mother responsible for her deficiency and never forgives her, reacting with an intense sense of loss and injury.

5. D. H. Hwang, *M. Butterfly* (New York: Plume, 1989).

6. Self-blame is a central issue in working with ambivalence. The question unexplored until now, however, is how to address the issue of self-blame when a person's loss is ambiguous and cannot be resolved.

7. S. Spielberg, *ET: The Extra-Terrestrial,* Universal City Studios, 1982.

8. B. D. Miller and B. L. Wood, "Childhood asthma in interaction with family, school and peer systems: A developmental model for pri-mary care," *Journal of Asthma,* 28 (1991): 405–414; B. D. Miller and B. L. Wood, "Influence of specific emotional states on autonomic reac-tivity and pulmonary function in asthmatic children," *Journal of the American Academy of Child and Adolescent Psychiatry,* 36:5 (1997): 669–677.

5. Ups and Downs

1. P. Boss, *Family Stress Management* (Newbury Park, Calif.: Sage Publications, 1988, rev. ed. 1999). This work was based on the earlier work of the family stress theorist and sociologist Reuben Hill.

2. D. Fravel and P. Boss, "An in-depth interview with the parents of missing children," in J. Gilgun, K. Daly, G. Handel, eds., *Qualitative Methods in Family Research* (Newbury Park, Calif.: Sage Publications, 1992), pp. 126–145.

3. S. Fisher and R. L. Fisher, *The Psychology of Adaptation to Absurdity* (Hillsdale, N.J.: Lawrence Erlbaum Associates, 1993), p. 183.

4. C. Middlebrook, *Seeing the Crab* (New York: Basic Books, 1996), p. 211.

5. Fravel and Boss, "An in-depth interview," p. 140.

6. Ibid., p. 136.

7. P. Boss and D. Riggs, *The Family and Alzheimer's Disease: Ambiguous Loss* (Minneapolis: University of Minnesota Media Productions, 1987).

8. Ibid.

6. The Family Gamble

1. Records of Mateo Sabog (Washington, D.C., Vietnam Memorial, National Park Service). Newspaper accounts spelled Mr. Sabog's first name incorrectly, as "Matheus," according to the ranger with whom I spoke. On the wall, his name is spelled Mateo Sabog. While there are some other soldiers mistakenly listed as dead on the wall, Mateo Sabog is the only one listed there whose family did not know that he was alive.

2. *Losing It All* (HBO Production, Time-Warner Productions, Inc., 1991), written, edited, and produced by M. Meirendorf.

3. C. R. Figley, ed., *Mobilization, Part I: The Iranian Crisis. Final Report of the Task Force on Families of Catastrophe* (West LaFayette, Ind.: Purdue University Family Research Institute Press, 1980).

4. For their accounts, see http://www.net4tv.com/color/80/iran-host.htm.

5. *Losing It All.*

6. Ibid.

7. Ibid.

8. E. Goffman, *Frame Analysis* (New York: Harper and Row,

148

1974). Goffman says that death is one event that has a frame, and that individuals are therefore not expected to decide on the status of a family member as alive or dead. He was wrong.

9. J. Powers, *Boston Globe Magazine,* March 10, 1996, p. 5.

10. George Herbert Mead was a pioneer in the social psychology of interpersonal meaning. See G. H. Mead, *On Social Psychology: Selected Papers,* ed. Anselm Strauss (Chicago: University of Chicago Press, 1934).

11. S. Tamaro, *Follow Your Heart* (New York: Doubleday, 1994), p. 56.

7. The Turning Point

1. D. Reiss, *The Family's Reconstruction of Reality* (Cambridge, Mass.: Harvard University Press, 1981).

2. William F. Buckley's interview with Mother Teresa (PBS, July 13, 1989).

3. Family meetings were used as an intervention at the Veterans Administration Hospital in Minneapolis as part of my NIA research with Alzheimer's caregivers. I also use family meetings in my private practice with families of chronically mentally ill patients. In family therapy circles, this method is considered a psycho-educational approach combined with symbolic experiential and narrative traditions.

4. See R. V. Speck and C. L. Attneave, *Family Networks* (New York: Pantheon, 1973). Carolyn Attneave, a Native American family therapist, wrote that "every culture contains all the possible values. The contrasts are not between opposites but between preferences and priorities" (p. 62).

8. Making Sense out of Ambiguity

1. C. B. Avery, ed., *The New Century Classical Handbook* (New York: Appleton-Century-Crofts, Inc., 1962), p. 1015. See also A. Camus, *The Myth of Sisyphus and Other Essays,* trans. Justin O'Brien (New York: Vintage Books, 1955), p. 90.

2. P. Boss, L. Kaplan, and M. Gordon, "Accepting the circle of life,"

Center for Urban and Regional Affairs Reporter, 25, 3 (1995): 7–11; **149** see also P. Boss, "Family values and belief systems," in *Family Stress Management* (Newbury Park, Calif.: Sage Publications, 1988), pp. 95–108, and discussion on just-world theory, pp. 118 and 127–129.

3. M. E. P. Seligman, *Learned Optimism* (New York: Pocket Books, 1990). See his description of depressed mood: "A pessimistic explanatory style is at the core of depressed thinking . . ." (p. 58). See also p. 5.

4. J. Smiley, *One Thousand Acres* (New York: Fawcett Columbine Books, 1991), p. 235.

5. D. Fravel and P. Boss, "An in-depth interview with the parents of missing children," in J. Gilgun, K. Daly, G. Handel, eds., *Qualitative Methods in Family Research* (Newbury Park, Calif.: Sage Publications, 1992), pp. 140–141.

6. C. Jung, *Memories, Dreams, and Reflections* (New York: Pantheon Books, 1961), p. 340.

7. K. Asmal, L. Asmal, and R. S. Roberts, *Reconciliation through Truth* (New York: St. Martin's Press, 1997).

8. See A. Antonovsky, *Health, Stress and Coping* (San Francisco: Jossey-Bass, 1979); A. Antonovsky, *Unraveling the Mystery of Health* (San Francisco: Jossey-Bass, 1987); P. L. Berger and T. Luckmann, *The Social Construction of Reality* (New York: Anchor Books, 1966); J. Patterson and A. Garwick, "Levels of meaning in family stress theory," *Family Process,* 33 (1994): 287–304; V. Frankl, *Man's Search for Meaning* (New York: Touchstone, Simon and Schuster, 1984). See also A. Miller, "The empty chair," in *Collected Plays* (New York: Viking, 1957), p. 8. Miller wrote about the universal themes of loss, aborted grieving, and meaning.

9. R. Akutagawa, "In a grove," in *Rashomon and Other Stories* (Rutland, Vt., and Tokyo: Charles E. Tuttle Company, 1952), pp. 13–25. This is a Zen story about the balance of illusion and reality.

10. Antoine de Saint-Exupéry, trans. Katherine Woods, *The Little Prince* (New York: Harcourt Brace Jovanovich, 1971), p. 83.

11. Ibid., pp. 86–87.

12. Scientists do not deny meaning or its importance in avoiding human suffering; medical researchers increasingly document that meaning

150 influences health. See, for example, B. D. Miller and B. L. Wood, "Influence of specific emotional states on autonomic reactivity and pulmonary function in asthmatic children," *Journal of the American Academy of Child and Adolescent Psychiatry*, 36:5 (1997): 669– 677; A. Antonovsky, *Health, Stress and Coping* (San Francisco: Jossey-Bass, 1979); A. Antonovsky, *Unraveling the Mystery of Health* (San Francisco: Jossey-Bass, 1987); and A. Ellenberger, *The Discovery of the Unconscious* (New York: Basic Books, 1970). Ellenberger writes of a patient named Frank who was in the coronary care unit with excruciating chest pain. The patient believed it was caused by a heart attack. To relieve his boredom, he learned how to control his blood pressure. Upon discharge, Dr. Ellenberger asked him how he was able to do it. "I do it with meaning," he said. "If I want my heart rate to fall, I close my eyes and focus on the chest pain. I let it mean to me that it's only indigestion or perhaps muscle pain. I know it's nothing; I'll be back to work tomorrow. If I want to increase the heart rate, I switch the meaning. I think the worst; I've had a real heart attack. I'll never get back to work. I'm just waiting around for the big one." Quoted in L. Dossey, *Alternative Therapies*, vol. 1, no. 3 (July 1995), p. 10. Frank's case illustrates that meanings can make a difference in stress levels and medical outcomes.

9. The Benefit of a Doubt

1. *The Letters of John Keats*, ed. M. B. Forman, 4th ed. (London: Oxford, 1952), p. 71. Keats defines "negative capability" as "when [one] is capable of being in uncertainties, Mysteries, doubts without any irritable reaching after fact and reason." See also A. Walker, *Anything We Love Can Be Saved* (New York: Random House, 1997).

2. E. Pulleyblank and T. Valva, *My Symptom Is Stillness: An ALS Story* (Berkeley, Calif.: East Bay Media Center, 1991); E. Pulleyblank, "Hard lessons," *The Family Therapy Networker* (Jan./Feb. 1996), pp. 42–49, and personal communication, Sept. 1998.

3. V. Frankl, *Man's Search for Meaning* (New York: Touchstone, 1984).

4. G. Radner, *It's Always Something* (New York: Avon Books, 1989), pp. 267–268. "Delicious ambiguity" was a term her support

group leader, Joanna Bull, used with cancer patients at the Wellness   **151**
Center in Santa Monica.

5. S. Fisher and R. L. Fisher, *The Psychology of Adaptation to Absurdity* (Hillsdale, N.J.: Lawrence Erlbaum Associates, 1993), p. 183. See also D. Brissett and C. Edgley, *Life As Theater* (Chicago: Aldine Pub. Co., 1975), p. 107.

6. R. Toner, *New York Times*, Feb. 9, 1996, section A, p. 24, column 1.

7. J. Schindler, *How to Live 365 Days a Year* (Englewood Cliffs, N.J.: Prentice-Hall, Inc., 1954).

Acknowledgments

Since 1974 I have been a marital and family therapist and teacher, and have conducted research at two land-grant universities known for upholding empiricism—the University of Wisconsin-Madison and the University of Minnesota. But it was my year at Judge Baker Children's Center in Boston that rekindled my interest in narrative analysis and the value of listening to people's stories. For the 1996 academic year I was a visiting professor of psychology in the department of psychiatry, Harvard Medical School, at the Judge Baker Children's Center. I am deeply indebted to Stuart Hauser, the president of the center and professor of psychiatry, Harvard Medical School, for making that year—and thus this book—possible. I also thank my colleagues at Judge Baker and in Cambridge who provided new insights. My thanks are also due to the National Institute of Mental Health post-doctoral trainees who helped to galvanize my own thinking as we discussed their family research.

Living in Cambridge during the year I spent at Judge Baker Children's Center provided me with the setting I needed to write this book. Moving there would not have been possible without the generous support of the Bush Foundation in the form of a Bush Sabbatical Award.

During the summer of 1996, I also visited McGill Univer-

154   sity in Montreal, where I listened to Cree and Inuit therapists and graduate students. For making this possible, and for their helpful comments on ambiguous loss, I thank Laurence Kirmayer, the director of the Division of Transcultural Psychiatry and professor of psychiatry, McGill University, and Herta Guttman, the psychiatrist-in-chief of the Royal Victoria Hospital and professor of psychiatry, McGill University.

The research and clinical work upon which this book is based spans the years 1973 to the present. I am deeply grateful to those who gave early support to testing an idea that grew out of my clinical observations, and, I now know, my personal experience. Financial support for the research on ambiguous loss from physical absence was provided by the U.S. Naval Health Research Institute, Center for Prisoner of War Studies (Family Branch), in San Diego; the University of Wisconsin-Madison Graduate School; the University of Wisconsin Experiment Station; and since 1981 the University of Minnesota Experiment Station and the Department of Family Social Science.

My research on ambiguous loss from psychological absence was funded from 1986 to 1991 by the National Institute on Aging, project grant no. 1-POI-AG-06309-01, project no. 5: "The Psychosocial Impact of Dementia on the Family and Caregiver of Alzheimer's Disease Patients," for which I was the principal investigator; the University of Minnesota Experiment Station; the Department of Family Social Science; and the University of Minnesota Graduate School. This research was conducted in cooperation with the Veterans Administration Hospital in Minneapolis.

The research project entitled "Caregiver Well-Being in Native American Families with Dementia" was funded by the

University of Minnesota All-University Council on Aging, 1992–1993. The University of Minnesota Experiment Station and the Department of Family Social Science also provided funds for this project.

For reading early drafts and offering insights that helped make this book possible I am grateful to my colleagues David Reiss, Jan Goldman, Beatrice Wood, John DeFrain, Terrence Williams, Wayne Caron, Deborah Lewis Fravel, Joyce Piper, and Lori Kaplan; and graduate students Raksha Dave Gates, Ciloue Cheng Stewart, Cary Sherman, and Kevin Doll. I also thank Sungeun Yang, who provided technical expertise in preparing the final manuscript. I am indebted to my editor, Elizabeth Knoll, who saved me from myself when I veered off the track into academic jargon and theoretical intricacies.

I am profoundly grateful to all the individuals and families I have learned from over the years. They have taught me to see and not just to theorize abstractly. With deep love and appreciation, I especially thank my mother, Verena Magdalena Grossenbacher-Elmer, who at eighty-seven continues to live in her own home in southern Wisconsin, where she remains actively involved with family, friends, church, and community. When I go to visit her, I see my father's paintings on every wall, my grandmother's needlework in every room, and my sister's photos, all too recent, on every table. These are reminders of those absent in my family; but through such symbols of their presence, my children, grandchildren, and I experience a sense of pride and stability in spite of change.

Finally, I thank my husband, Dudley Riggs, who from his own experience knew how to support me as I wrote, and did so without ambiguity.